AF271052

IN GOOD HANDS

by

Joey Jones

EDITED BY

Darryal W. Ray

Huntsville
ALBRIGHT & COMPANY 1985

*Dedicated to four who made
a difference* —

Mary Jones
Elise Lapeyre Jones
Ray Perkins
Paul W. Bryant (1913-1983)

Acknowledgements

Photographs courtesy of the University of Alabama Sports Information Department; Stephen Gross, Karen Elkins and Chuck Slaton of the *Anniston Star;* Joel Salcido of the *El Paso Times;* *'Bama Magazine;* Jimmy Mills of First Alabama Bank; Mary Jones and Elise Lapeyre Jones.

And a very special thanks to . . . J. D. Rutledge for his invaluable cooperation; WUAL Radio of Tuscaloosa for tapes and research assistance; Gilbert E. Johnston, Jr., for a lawyer's careful read; the Birmingham Stallions and Hal Hayes for statistical updates; Clyde Bolton and Tommy Ford for their expertise; John Eaton and the Georgia Volunteer Lawyers for the Arts for direction and sound legal advice; Coaches Al Miller and Jack Rutledge for filling in the gaps; *The Anniston Star* for its many indulgences and kindness; Charles Goldberg for his time and editing skills; Kirk McNair for his generosity; Fran Viselli for the missing poem; Rev. Joe Elmore for Coach Bryant's eulogy; David McMakin for his faith and a second chance; and last but not least, Judy Ray for her support, her understanding and a wife's gentle push.

**Editor's Forward

There comes a time in every profession when you need to hang it up, and that time has come for me as head football coach at the University of Alabama. . .

— Paul 'Bear' Bryant

December 15, 1982

He was 20 years old and in the grip of a mid-life crisis. He was confused, angry, and resentful.

Joey Jones was caught in The Change.

This is the story of that change.

It is not a story about Coach Paul "Bear" Bryant, a man who became a legend long before he became the winningest coach in the history of college football. It is not a story about Coach Ray Perkins, a former player under Bryant who dared follow in the footsteps of a legend. And it is not a story about Joey Jones, the diminutive split end who defied all odds to become one of the most popular players to ever wear the uniform of the Alabama Crimson Tide.

It is, instead, a story about all three of these men and others whose lives became entwined in the struggle to keep Alabama's football dynasty from crumbling.

It was not intended to be this way. When Joey and I first met in October 1982, it was because we felt a book—or diary if you will—of Joey's career at Alabama may be of great interest to college football fans. Coach Bryant's resignation and death and Coach Perkins' appointment as head coach were unforeseen factors that ultimately changed the book's course. And although those were difficult times for Joey, they made the book what it is.

Ironically, it was because of Coach Bryant that I feared Joey would initially decline my offer to do the book. Instead, Joey eagerly accepted the idea as a means of remembering his beloved coach.

"There has been so much to happen to me here," Joey said, "and I want to remember all of it. A book is the best way to do that."

I did not argue. I provided Joey with an outline of things to watch for, an armload of blank cassette tapes, and two tape recorders—a large one to keep in his room at Bryant Hall, and a smaller one to fit into his coat pocket. Still, I did not want to jeopardize Joey's playing career at Alabama or to cause any undue reprisal against him. So it was agreed that nothing he reported on tape would be published until after his college eligibility expired.

He did not let me down. He talked into his tape recorders for well over a year, revealing Alabama football as never before. His humor was refreshing, his honesty alarming. By the time he signed a three-year contract with the Birmingham Stallions of the United States Football League, Joey had used enough tape to stretch from Tuscaloosa to his home in Mobile several times over. The task of transcribing and editing those tapes fell on me, but it was a pleasurable chore.

I cannot say that we agreed on everything. Joey is an optimist at heart, and it is my failing to be somewhat of a pessimist. So when I once challenged his positive viewpoint of a particular incident, Joey replied, "If we're going to be honest about it, that's the way it's got to be because that's how I feel." He had me there. That is not to say, however, that this book is another "fluff piece"—full of rah rah for the old U of A. It is not. It is, we think an honest look at life in Bryant Hall at a time when Alabama's football future was in question. Of course, when one tells the truth, one sometimes offends. It was not our intent to offend— only to tell the truth.

The use of profanity was another decision we had to make. I did not want the book to read like a Bobbsey Twins primer. To do so would make even the truth sound unbelievable. By the same token, Joey did not want the book to read like bathroom graffiti. So we settled for somewhere in between. The result is a "PG" rating.

Despite Joey's wonderful cooperation, this was not an easy book for either of us to do. There were times when Joey's conscience bothered him. "I just don't feel right thinking about the book when I should be thinking about the game," he once confided. And although his reluctance to tape team meetings may have cost us a valuable piece of history, it only added to the book's sincerity.

Still, it pained me to listen to those tapes when Joey fought back tears to tell of Coach Bryant's resignation. And when I heard his delayed report on Coach Bryant's death, I felt ashamed for putting Joey through it all again. Joey was so shaken by Coach Bryant's death that the book project was almost abandoned. But Joey is a fighter, and he bounced back just as he has done so many times on the playing field.

It was all part of being caught in The Change.

Darryal Ray
Anniston, Alabama 1984

Editor's Note

Because football uniforms do not have pockets, it was not possible for Joey Jones to carry a tape recorder with him at all times. Therefore, some conversations by players and coaches contained herein are not necessarily verbatim accounts of certain events, but instead, are Joey's recollection of those conversations. To the best of Joey's knowledge, they are accurate. It is also possible some events may not correspond with the date(s) given.

Contents

Introduction: Fall 1982

I am 5-foot-9, I weigh 168 pounds soaking wet, and I play football for the University of Alabama.

Honest.

I know that's hard to believe. Sometimes, I don't believe it myself. When I walk into the dressing room before a practice and sit down next to offensive linemen almost a foot taller and a hundred pounds heavier than I, I wonder if I have taken a wrong turn ("Little people, next room please"). Linemen always seem to have the macho nicknames— "Hoss," "Big John," or "Biceps" just to name a few. Know what they call me around here? "Little Big Man." You don't frighten too many linebackers with that nickname.

But actually, my size has never bothered me. I was never particularly offended by Randy Newman's song *Short People.* I never stuffed toilet paper into the heels of my shoes just to look taller, and I don't mind having to tiptoe to see into the huddle.

I don't think of myself as "short"—I'm just "not tall." But for what I lack in height, I make up with speed. During spring drills, I ran the 40-yard dash in 4.42 seconds. That wasn't even my best time, but it was fast enough that the coaches who were timing me thought their stop watch was broken. I can still out-run anybody on the whole squad. It's a matter of survival, always has been.

When I was about seven or eight, I spent many fall afternoons playing football with my friends in the park across the street from my house in Mobile. Well, actually it wasn't football—it was a game we called "pick up and smear." Survival is the only rule of "smear." One guy kicks the football as high into the air as he can, and when the ball hits the ground, you pick it up and run like crazy. Because if you don't run like crazy, the other guys will "smear" your body all over the park. I didn't get "smeared" often.

Real football requires more than speed, however. It took only one play as a 124-pound tailback on the Murphy High junior varsity to realize I was not cut out to be a running back. So I tried quarterback for one year, and although I did all right, it just wasn't for me. By the time I made the varsity, I had found a home as wide receiver. I've been there ever since.

So, you see, size isn't my problem—it's everyone else's problem. I always have to do things a little better, run a little faster, jump a little higher to convince others that I can play football with the big boys. I admit that it can be frustrating. It took more than a year to convince Coach Paul "Bear" Bryant that I could play. But it was well worth the wait.

Sometimes people ask why I bother with football, why I spend most of my free time getting knocked down by gorillas wearing football helmets, why I enjoy getting turf burns on my elbows. I am really not sure why I do it. I guess it's because I enjoy it, and I enjoy winning—that wonderful sense of accomplishing something. And I guess it's because I have enough ham in me that I enjoy the small measure of fame that accompanies winning and wearing that crimson jersey.

I am now a junior, and although we have missed our chance of bringing the national championship to Alabama in 1982, I still have dreams that it will soon happen again.

I dream that it's January and the New Orleans Superdome is filled to capacity with 'Bama pennants, placards and houndstooth hats. My mother is sitting in the stands with my girlfriend and a couple of friends from high school. Everyone is cheering for me.

My heart is pumping and my palms are sweating. I want the football. And sometimes in these dreams, I get it.

I can see the score is tied, the national title on the line, and time is running out. My number is called, the ball snapped, and I break for the goal posts. I turn my head, but the lights are in my eyes and a defensive back is shadowing me. I reach out and grip the ball with my fingertips—touchdown! My teammates rush onto the field and lift me on their shoulders. Coach Bryant hugs me and says, "I knew you could do it, Little Man." He retires my jersey right on the spot. I make national headlines, and I am the cover boy on all the national sports magazines. The Associated Press names me Amateur Athlete of the Year.

Of course, it is only a dream. But who is to say it can't happen? Because in my lifetime, I have learned it's not whether you are short or tall, it's how you play the game.

PART I

At Low Tide

November 24, 1982
Bryant Hall

Joe Namath came to the rescue today and brought the whole darn cavalry with him. It wasn't an accident.

It wasn't like ol' Broadway Joe just happened to be flying through the neighborhood and decided to drop in to see how the old school was doing. Otherwise, I don't believe Lee Roy Jordan, Wilbur Jackson, Major Ogilvie and anybody else who ever played football for "The Bear" would have come too. But they did—every last one of them. No, this has to be Coach Bryant's idea, another ploy to get our minds back on the winning track. The Old Motivator has been working overtime again.

Actually, it's not that unusual for Coach Bryant to bring in ex-jocks, politicians, and other celebrity types when he thinks we are slipping. And believe me, we have been slipping.

This was supposed to be *our* season. The newspaper polls and pre-season magazines all agreed that winning a national championship would be a cinch for the University of Alabama this season. The sad thing is they were right. It *should* have been a snap. We had (and still have) everything going for us—talent, coaching, schedule. The works.

We were going to mix a little "I" formation offense in with the wishbone, the defense was going to kick some tails, and we were going to gift-wrap a national championship in a neat, tidy little package for Coach Bryant.

So what do we do? For starters, we're now looking at a 7-3 record, we've stunk up the Southeastern Conference, we've had to settle for a Liberty Bowl invitation againt Illinois on December 29, and we've just about convinced the winningest football coach of all time that he is in the wrong line of work.

We've set all kinds of records—all the wrong ones. Seven-and-three is the worst record for an Alabama team in 12 years. Our third loss—a 38-29 loss to Southern Mississippi just 11 days ago—happened in Bryant-Denny Stadium in front of God and everybody. It was the first loss in Tuscaloosa since 1963. I've never been so embarrassed in my life.

That's why I think Namath and his band of former Tide superstars have arrived too late. The damage has already been done. We're picking up the pieces and we've somehow managed to get our minds back on business without anybody's help.

In three days, we close out the regular season against Auburn. I don't have to tell you what that means. Around here you might be able to get away with losing to LSU once every hundred years. You might even be able to lose to Tennessee every thousand years. But lose to Auburn, and you had better change your address quickly. That's why we're taking this game so seriously. The fact that Auburn fans have sent us letters about how they plan to tear down the goal posts after *they* win only makes us work that much harder.

Today's practice was the best all season. Our quarterback, Walter Lewis, was running the wishbone like clockwork. The offensive line could have held back the New York Sack Exchange. And the defense was playing with fire in their eyes.

Of course, Namath's presence may have had something to do with it. I'll be the first to admit I was showing off some because I knew Namath was on the sidelines. I didn't try anything fancy, nothing stupid like that. I just put on my give-'em-hell-on-Saturday smile, bowed my neck, and went to work. I wanted Namath to see that Alabama's passing game did not die out with the 1960s. I cut corners faster than I cut finance classes; I made the defensive backs look almost silly (but only almost) a couple of times on the sideline fakes; and I snatched passes out of the air like I was wearing gloves made from flypapaer. Shoot, I even pretended not to notice when two defensive backs nailed me to the ground on a slant pattern across the middle. I went one way, the ball another way, and I could hear the harps play "Swing Low, Sweet Chariot." My head was still ringing when I suddenly realized that I wasn't the only guy out there who was trying to impress Namath. Everybody wanted to look good.

But Dante Bramblett had one up on everybody.

Dante, a linebacker from Morrow, Georgia, was feeling especially important today. I can't say that I blame him. It seems that Dante and Namath had once dated the same girl—a fact that Dante obviously took great pride in. Ol' Dante was strutting around like the only rooster in the henhouse and pretending that he wasn't *all* that impressed by Namath. But if football jerseys had buttons, Dante would have burst all of them right off.

"I guess Joe and I just know how to pick 'em," he'd say and grin. "Hell, Joe probably wants *my* autograph!"

Of course, what made all this so much fun was that most of the guys did not believe Dante. Or if they did believe him, it was too much fun acting as if they didn't.

"Suuurre, Dante, suuurre," they'd say.

"It's true!" Dante would argue.

After watching Dante struggle with his credibility a few minutes, I broke down and told the others that it was true, that I knew the girl and that she was definitely All-NFL material. So, Dante triumphed in his greatest hour. A star was born.

Namath had come to watch us, but it wasn't long before the tables were turned and we were watching him. We especially admired his flair for fashion—designer jeans and a tailored mink jacket. Some of the guys even began playing a guessing game on how much the jacket cost.

"Whaddaya think? 15 thou?"

"Naw, man, not that much. More like 10 grand."

Heck, for all we knew about mink and furs, Namath's jacket could have been made out of 'possum skins.

Lee Roy Jordan had brought his sons along, and Namath was throwing passes to one of the boys on the sidelines. I was about seven years old when Namath was making headlines in the old American Football League, so you can imagine how I felt when I saw him play catch with this kid. It made me want to run over, push the kid aside, and say, "My turn, Joe! Throw me one!" Of course, that would have gone over about as well as singing "War Eagle" in the huddle, so I fought the urge. Besides, I would have been so nervous I couldn't have caught a cold.

I really don't know much about Alabama teams of the 1960s

because I wasn't born until Namath's freshman year here. (Yes, folks, it *has* been that long.) I do remember when Namath made his famous promise to Jets fans a few days before New York played Baltimore in the 1969 Super Bowl. New York was a 17-point underdog the week of the game, but Namath guaranteed the Jets would win. But if he had not come through and beat the Colts 16-7, Namath would have never made it on Broadway, or anywhere else for that matter.

Namath must be pushing 40 now. And if you can look past that giant schnoz (only slightly larger than my own), you can see a few wrinkles around his eyes. He is still so stoop-shouldered that he reminds me of those Neanderthal men you see in fourth grade textbooks. But his passing form is still picture perfect. It's just too bad his knees died 10 years ago. . . I'd love to sneak him into the Auburn game.

Namath is, of course, a legend in Alabama football. And because he is, I can't help feeling as if we have let him and the others down by having the kind of season we have had.

The bad part is that it all started out so well . . .

We opened against Georgia Tech in Atlanta. It was Coach Bryant's 69th birthday, and since Tech had beaten us two years ago, we were hungry. We scored the first five times we touched the ball and beat Tech 45-7. After the game, Coach Bryant made his traditional walk to the middle of the field to shake hands with Tech coach Bill Curry. But Curry would have no part of it. He jerked away and apparently exchanged words with Coach Bryant without realizing ESPN's television cameras were rolling. But we weren't being greedy. We were just working on some plays that we hadn't had a chance to practice on very much. So what if they did work *too* well? If we had wanted, we probably could have beaten Tech 145-7. The "I" worked that well, even if the only pass thrown to me was way too short.

The next weekend we went to Jackson, Mississippi, and beat Ole Miss 42-14 in weather so hot that most of us got sunburned. We were throwing more, but I was enjoying it less. It seemed like Jesse Bendross, our wide receiver, was getting *all* the passes. Only one pass was thrown to me and I got 33 yards out of it. I started wondering if the coaches didn't trust me.

Things got better for me against Vanderbilt the next weekend. I caught four passes for 80 yards and we beat them 24-

21. But beating Vandy by three points in Tuscaloosa didn't set well with our critics. That's when the fans first began complaining. The Associated Press dropped us from fourth to fifth because we didn't cover the point spread. But I don't care what you say—Vandy is a good team.

You can say what you like about Arkansas State. A lot of the guys on the team thought we were playing Arkansas of the Lou Holtz and Razorback variety until they saw the scouting report. The only reason they were on our schedule was because Coach Bryant was doing their coach, Larry Lacewell, a favor. Some favor, huh? We beat them 34-7 even though we fumbled the ball eight times. Plus, I caught two touchdown passes 23 seconds apart, one 20 yards and the other 71. My paranoia was beginning to disappear.

I think Arkansas State was a little intimidated by Legion Field because it has more seats than there are people in State University, Arkansas. I mean, when you see a team walking around the field before kickoff with cameras strapped around their necks and snapping pictures of the stadium, you *know* they've got to be impressed by something.

We took a lot of criticism from fans for having Arkansas State on our schedule, but that just made us work that much harder for Penn State the next weekend. The Penn State game was the most fun we've had all year, mainly because we won 42-21. It's always fun playing on national TV, but when you have a chance to look good on TV against a team with Penn State's reputation, it makes it even more fun. And we looked very good.

Winning that game gave us more confidence and silenced our critics. At last, we had beaten a good team, a somebody. AP moved us up to No. 2 in the poll, and the national championship seemed only a hop, skip and jump away. All we had to do was smooth things out—or so we thought.

I still get goose bumps when I think back to what Coach Bryant had said to us in practice a week before we played Penn State.

"If you think Penn State is tough," he had told us, "just wait until we play Tennessee."

The man is a psychic, I tell you. He knew something none of us knew, and had tried to warn us. We should have listened. But we were 5-and-0 and not terribly concerned about a team that was 2-2-1 and had not beaten us since 1970. After all, we *were* the No. 2 team in the nation!

It took only one play to change all that. Tennessee beat us 35-28 after intercepting Walter Lewis' pass in the end zone as time ran out. I can go back and randomly select a dozen plays in that game, and any of them could be the reason we lost. But the fans saw only one—Walter's interception. The really sad part about all this is that Walter played one heckuva game. He had 79 yards rushing and 200 passing. Still, that one interception turned a lot of fans against the team, and against Walter in particular.

Before that game, all the fans thought Walter was the best quarterback in the world—he could run, he could throw, and best of all, he had just beaten Penn State. But after that one interception, Walter suddenly became the worst quarterback in the world.

When we returned from Knoxville, all we could hear was, "What's wrong with Alabama?" Strangers were walking up to me and saying, "Ya'll have blown it now! Ya'll were No. 2, and now, ya'll have lost the national championship."

We didn't blow anything but one lousy game. Just one lousy game. And if we had been better able to handle the flack that came our way after the Tennessee loss, I honestly believe we could be 9-1 right now.

But some fans can't admit that we just got beat. They have to find a scapegoat. And they found one ready-made in Walter.

That was only logical. After all, Walter *is* the first black athlete to start at quarterback here. And Alabama *is* the school where George Wallace made his infamous stand in the schoolhouse door. So, it came as no surprise when rumors of racial problems began.

The first rumor we heard was that Walter was dating a white girl. After that, the rumors just snowballed. And they're still coming. Of course, none are true.

The popular theory now is that the offensive line refuses to block for Walter because he has this supposed relationship with a white girl. Plus there have been rumors that Russ Wood, our defensive end, and/or Tommy Wilcox, our safety, have had fights with Walter on the field or in the showers. The stories get more ridiculous from week to week. We sit around guessing what the next lie is going to be.

At first, we tried to laugh it off to keep things loose.

"Hey, Walter!" somebody would say, "You going out with that white girl tonight?"

"Yeah, man," Walter would say and smile. "I thought I'd take her dancing. You know how those white folks love to dance."

But now the jokes are wearing thin and Walter doesn't laugh so much at our wisecracks. You can see it in his eyes—it's bothering him. He tries to hide it, but you can tell he's hurting inside. I sympathize with him. It's tough enough being a quarterback at any school, but being a black quarterback at Alabama—well, that's really tough.

Somehow we managed to pick ourselves up well enough to beat Cincinnati 21-3 on homecoming. And even under the gun, Walter rushed 21 times for 156 yards and hit on six of seven passes for another 61 yards before hurting his shoulder in the fourth quarter.

The next weekend we returned to Jackson, Mississippi, and beat Mississippi State 20-12. I had the best game of my career—four passes for 103 yards and the go-ahead touchdown on a high pass betweeen two defensive backs. And Walter, by the way, passed for 171 yards. Things were clicking for us again—until we ran smack dab into LSU at Birmingham.

LSU ate us alive. The score was 20-10 and we were lucky it wasn't worse. Their defensive game plan was the best I've seen. I don't know if LSU saw something in the way Walter was positioning his feet or what, but LSU guessed right on almost every play and Walter spent half the day on his back. It wasn't a very pretty sight.

In the locker room after the game everyone was crying quietly. We had been whipped and we knew it. As usual, Coach Bryant tried to take the blame.

"You deserve better coaching than what I gave today," he said. "I should have prepared you better."

But nobody really believed him. We sat there staring at our shoelaces while he took the blame. We were accustomed to Coach Bryant taking the blame for our mistakes, but we were not prepared for what he told the press after he left the dresing room.

"I'm going to alert the [university] president and anybody else who wants to know, in a heckuva hurry, that we need to make some changes, need to start at the top," he told the press.

When the sportswriters came into the dressing room and started asking us about what Coach Bryant had said, we didn't know what to think. We sure as heck didn't want *him* to retire because *we* had screwed things up.

It was like the whole world was crumbling around us. In a sense, it was. That loss took us out of the running for the SEC championship. And, of course, another loss required another excuse. This time the fans blamed Mal Moore, our offensive coordinator. But it wasn't his fault—nothing could have kept LSU off of us that day.

We were all relieved when Coach Bryant announced a few days later that he would like to continue as head coach until "I'm 80 or 90—as long as I can get results."

Well, we let the old man down again against Southern Miss. But he hasn't said anything more about retiring. Besides, he's just 69. So, if he is coaching until he's 80, we'll have him at least 11 more years.

Now that you see what we've been through, maybe you will understand why some players have developed what our coaches call an "attitude problem." That's what the coaches said about Kenny Simon, Charlie Williams and Earl Collins, three of our running backs. All three were kicked off the team a few days ago and have since been exiled to Paty Hall (where the food is terrible, but the curfew can't be beat).

When someone is booted, you never hear it from the coaches. You may not even realize they are gone until they have missed a few days of practice, and then you see their locker is empty. But if the player is a starter or a top reserve, some sort of explanation is required to quell the public's curiosity.

In the case of Kenny, Charlie and Earl, Coach Bryant issued a press statement out of the sports information office that said they ". . . didn't have a winning attitude and should devote more time to their studies . . ."

Now when a coach tells you to devote more time to your studies, you *know* your head is on the old chopping block.

All three had been pretty unhappy about their lack of playing time, so it came as no real surprise. It wasn't the first time that Kenny Simon had gotten on Coach Bryant's bad side. He had been walking on eggs ever since that infamous episode when he allegedly fired a shotgun into the air to fighten two law students.

We kidded Kenny about that incident for awhile, and probably shouldn't have. He wanted to forget the whole thing, but nobody would let him live it down. We teased him about "hunting trips" and about "bag limits" on law students. Looking back on it now, I see that we were pretty cruel to him.

It's really a shame that this had to happen to them. All three were talented players and would have played more if they hadn't been hurt most of the time. But that's the way it is here—when you get hurt, the guy behind you is more than willing to take your place in line.

So that, in a rather large nutshell, is how our dream season has become a nighmare. And that, as I said before, is probably why Namath and Jordan and all those other guys came to practice today.

I know we can put it together again. I know we can beat Auburn. We showed that in practice today. It's just going to take some old-fashioned teamwork. Or, like Namath said, some "camaraderie." That was the word he used in the pep talk he gave us before practice ended.

Namath's accent is hard to follow. It has a bit of southern drawl, a little Beaver Falls, Pennsylvania, and a dash of California. But I hung onto his every word.

"I just want you guys to know that this game Saturday will be the most important game of your life," he said. "It's the one game that the fans won't let you forget—win or lose.

"I had the misfortune of losing to Auburn back in '63 and even now, everywhere I go, I find some Auburn fan there to remind me. They're going to hassle you about it for the rest of your lives.

"When I played here, we had a camaraderie that I'll always treasure. All the players were close. We had fun together. Even now, after all these years, whenever I meet an old teammate, we talk about the good time we had. And whenever we talk football, we think about that Auburn game and regret it because we lost.

"I hope you won't have to go through that."

Me neither, Joe, me neither.

With a hundred or so guys on a team, it's impossible to know everyone. Each year you have freshmen and walk-ons coming in, seniors graduating, and dozens of others quitting. I could probably look at our roster right now and not recognize 20 or 30 names on there.

Roommates are different, though. Mine is Paul Ott Carruth.

Paul is from Summitt, Mississippi, and a pretty good running back in my opinion. (I had to say that because he's listening to me make this tape. Just kidding!) Paul moved into my room two weeks after the Cotton Bowl game my sophomore year. He had been rooming with Chuckie Fields, but they had some kind of disagreement which Paul doesn't talk about, and Paul was wanting to move out. I don't know how he chose me, but I do know he was impressed with my room. As soon as he walked through the door that first day, he looked around the room and said, "Well, at least I know you'll be neat." Little did he know that he had caught me in a yearly cleaning binge. I had even made up my bed. Three weeks later, the room was a disaster area.

Paul doesn't talk much. I guess that comes from his Southern up-bringing—don't speak until you're spoken to. But he is a very good friend and has helped me though the important things in a college student's life, such as girls and cars and cars and girls.

Mike Adcock is another close friend. He is a 6-foot-2, 230-pound offensive guard from Huntsville. Mike is also the kind of guy who hates practice, hates team meetings, hates everything leading up to a game. But on Saturdays, he will be out there giving it his all and will usually end up grading higher than any of the offensive linemen.

I also count Mike White and Doug Vickers among my friends. They are roommates, and they have the best darn 21-inch color TV in Bryant Hall. I've spent many nights in their room watching *M*A*S*H* or Archie Bunker on their TV. Mike and Doug are about the same size (6-3, 250) and both are offensive linemen.

But the similarities stop there. Doug's hobby is eating—he inhales take-out pizza. Mike's hobby is rock 'n roll and lifting weights. They call Mike "Ceps" (short for biceps) because of his big muscles.

Then, there are the "name" players, the people you read

about in the newspapers. One is Linnie Patrick, a running back from Jasper's Walker High School. Linnie's entire career has been marked by controversy. That's a shame, too, because Linnie is really a great guy once you get to know him.

I think the trouble with Linnie is that people were expecting so much out of him when he signed with Alabama that he began believing his own press clippings. He was a *Parade* magazine All-American, and he had an incredible high school career. The trouble began just weeks after he signed. He was at the high school all-star game here when he was interviewed by some reporter. That turned out to be a mistake. Linnie is just too open, too honest, and yes, maybe even too full of himself to give interviews. He told the reporter he wanted to win the Heisman Trophy not once, but three times, after contending for it as a freshman. I can imagine how Coach Bryant reacted when he read that in the newspaper. Individual goals are not something you talk about at Alabama. Here, the team comes first, not the player.

But that was just the beginning. Linnie still has not won a Heisman, but he has probably set a record for team suspensions. If Linnie isn't breaking curfew, he's sneaking back home, or failing to go to the treatment room for an injury, or whatever. I heard the players describe Linnie as a "free soul." I think that fits him pretty well.

But Linnie can be great. He has unbelievable moves and can follow a blocking pattern probably better than anyone on the team. Last year, against Auburn, he carried the ball only four times but gained 48 yards and scored a touchdown. The next day Coach Bryant was quoted in the newspapers as saying, "What I wouldn't give to reach that young man." But just a few days later, Linnie broke curfew again and missed the trip to the Cotton Bowl.

Linnie is the only person I've ever seen who could make Coach Bryant mad—I mean *really* mad. Linnie had been just going through the motions one day in practice and Coach Bryant decided it was time Linnie had a "gut check."

Coach Bryant climbed down from his tower and headed straight for Coach Moore, who was directing the first team offense. Coach Bryant was steaming, and we could see it coming.

"Mal," Coach Bryant said, "give Linnie the ball."

"Yes sir," Coach Moore replied and called a play for Linnie

to run. The ball was snapped, Linnie took the handoff from Walter, ran about five steps, and was creamed by the defense.

"Give it to him again," Coach Bryant said.

So Coach Moore called another play, and again Linnie got the ball. And again the defense creamed him.

"Do it over!" Coach Bryant ordered.

Coach Moore obeyed. And again Linnie was pounded.

I don't know how many times Linnie got the ball that day, but I would guess it was around 18 straight times. But around the 18th time, Linnie was ready to drop. In fact, he did. After he was tackled, he just lay there resting.

"Get up!" Coach Bryant yelled.

Linnie didn't budge.

"Get up, Linnie!" Coach Bryant screamed.

Well, Linnie got up. But when he did, he was mad as hell. He threw his helmet across the field, walked to the sidelines and sat down. I was just beginning to wonder what Coach Bryant would do next when I saw him running—yes, *running*—straight toward Linnie. When he reached him, he jerked Linnie up by the jersey and began shaking him like a rag doll.

"You S.O.B.!" Coach Bryant screamed in Linnie's face. "You think you know it all, don't you! You think you're the best damn thing to ever come through here, don't you! Well, let me tell you something—you're not! You never have been and you never will be because you're a quitter! A damn quitter! You make me sick!"

Linnie sat there pouting the rest of the day while we practiced. He lost some friends that day because everybody was scared to be seen talking to him after that. But things have since cooled down, and we're all pulling for Linnie to make it.

Then, there's Jesse Bendross. I won't call Jesse our "other receiver" because that wouldn't be fair to him. Jesse is from Hollywood, Florida, and we first met at a summer camp at Florida State. We had just graduated from high school and were trying to decide on our college. FSU wanted us both, but we were slightly jealous of each other and didn't want to both end up at the same school. I figured Jesse was going to sign with Florida State, so I went ahead and signed with Alabama. You can imagine how I felt when I met Jesse in the hallway on the day I reported to Alabama. It was a bad reunion for both of us.

"Uh oh!" Jesse said, breaking into a wide grin. "I didn't know you were coming here."

"And I didn't know you were coming here, either," I said. He was trying to be nice, trying to make it sound like he was worried about me taking away his job. But I was the one who was worried. I was faster than Jesse, but he was bigger. And when Jesse moved into a starting job his freshman year when Keith Marks got hurt, I figured I was in for a long four years. I started thinking about transferring to FSU as early as then.

Although Jesse and I get about the same amount of playing time now (and about the same number of passes), I'd be lying if I said that there is still not some degree of rivalry between us. When Jesse thinks not enough passes are coming his way, he gets moody and pouts. When things don't go my way, I get mad because I think that the coaches don't like my height. And the only way I can combat that is to work harder and run faster.

Our game captain each week is Steve Mott, a center from New Orleans. Some people around Bryant Hall say that Mott is the most crude person on the team. At a team initiation his freshman year, Mott passed a jar around the room and requested that every person who dipped snuff to spit into the jar. Everyone wondered why until Mott raised the jar like a salute, and said, "Cheers!" He then guzzled down the entire contents of the jar. Mott's roomie, Ken Coley, says Steve is warped." I agree.

Another character is Joe Beazley, an offensive tackle from Virginia. If Beazley isn't the champion beer drinker on the team, he's at least the champion beer can collector. He must have 300 crushed beer cans under his bed at this very moment. He also has a love for strange animals. He makes pets out of any roaches he may find scampering around his room. He also has a small shark in his aquarium. The shark eats bacon—and other fish.

Steve Booker, a linebacker from Huntsville, is the team's tough guy. Or so he says. Booker is a good friend who enjoys topping you at everything. If you say you can jump 23 feet, Booker says he can jump 24. I guess that's why he loves to fight. Booker once told me that he's seen only one man tougher than he. That was Andra Franklin, a running back from Anniston who now plays for the Miami Dolphins.

"I played against Franklin when I was in high school," Booker said. "When I tried to tackle him, he carried my ass 80 yards for a touchdown. He's the baddest dude I ever saw in my life."

So I asked him, "Who's the second baddest dude you ever saw?"

"Oh," Booker said, "there was this guy in Huntsville who used to beat everybody up in the bars. I got into a fight with him one night."

"How did you do?" I asked.

"We tied," said Booker. I should have known.

Rocky Colburn is our practical joker. Rocky, a skinny defensive back from Atmore, will do anything for a laugh. One night after returning from some horror flick with Terry Sanders and Todd Roper, Rocky waited until Roper was sound asleep. Then he put on this bloody Halloween mask, got a huge butcher knife, and sneaked into Roper's room. He stood over Roper's bed, raised the knife over his head and let out a menacing scream. Roper sprung out of the bed and raced out of the room wearing only his Fruit of the Looms. Sanders and a half dozen others were waiting outside the door, rolling in laughter.

Then there's Jackie Cline, a defensive tackle from Birmingham whom we call Bucket Head because that's how he looks once he straps on his helmet. Jackie is the strong, silent type and he's as cuddly as a teddy bear off the field. In fact, when he first came here four years ago, Jackie was so afraid of hurting someone in practice that he was holding back. But after our defensive coordinator, Ken Donohue, kept him after practice a few days, Jackie learned that nice guys finish last on the football field.

Randy Edwards, another friend of mine, never had that problem. He's naturally mean—and naturally smart. Randy and I have a macroeconomics class together, and he amazes me with the way he studies. I can study for an exam for three days and make an 89. Randy can study an hour before the test and make a perfect 100. I'll never understand how he does it. The other day I noticed Randy sitting there doodling on his notebook. I looked closer. It was a drawing of a football player. Below the picture he had written, *"Auburn Quarterback."* Above the picture, Randy had written in big letters, *"KILL AUBURN!!!"* Yep, Randy's mean all right . . .

PART II

Auburn . . . and Other Jokes

November 25, 1982
Bryant Hall

An Auburn coach came home early from practice one day to find his wife in bed with one of his top players.

He was so angry that he rushed to his dresser and pulled out a gun. He pulled back the hammer and pointed the gun at his head.

His wife was so happy that she was going to be a rich widow that she immediately burst into laughter.

"I wouldn't laugh if I were you," the coach screamed. "You're next!"

Actually that's just an Auburn joke I overheard the other day. At least I think it was a joke.

I usually don't tell jokes because I screw up the punch lines and nobody laughs. But there is an exception to every rule, and Auburn week is the exception to this one.

Everybody tells Auburn jokes during the week of the Alabama-Auburn game. It's a tradition, which is another way of saying that your great-great-grandfather told the same jokes when he was a kid.

As a rule, Auburn jokes are pretty bad. They are without taste or class, don't always make sense, and generally deal with anything from pigs to cow manure or an Auburn student's low mentality. In other words, Auburn jokes are shamefully accurate. Yuk. Yuk.

They are also habit-forming. Hold on—I think I feel another one coming on. . .

"What do you call a pretty girl at Auburn?"

"A visitor."

Or how about this one. . .

"What do you call an Auburn coed who marries an Alabama football player?"

"A social climber."

Here's another one . . .

"What do you call an Auburn limousine?"

"A tractor."

Sorry folks, I can't help myself.

I hope I haven't given you the wrong impression. I don't hate Auburn. Honest. I do harbor a strong dislike for Auburn however. And yet, the dirtiest team that I've ever played against wasn't Auburn—it was Rutgers. Rutgers plays even dirtier football than Kentucky, and that's saying plenty. A Kentucky player may spit in your face at the line of scrimmage, but a Rutgers player will bite you first and *then* spit on the open wound. A game with Rutgers is like a street fight where there are only two rules: (1) don't get caught in the bottom of the pile, and (2) be sure to get your tetanus shots early. They are *that* mean. Rahway State Prison ain't got nothing on those guys from East Rutherford.

By comparison, Auburn players usually behave like gentlemen—no biting, no spitting, no piling on. Oh, there have been a few scattered incidents but nothing worth belly-aching about.

In fact, a lot of guys on the team have friends who play for Auburn. Some may even bring an Auburn player to *our* victory party after the game.

An Auburn player will help you up after he's knocked you on your butt, and he will shake your hand after you have embarrassed him on national TV. I know because I saw it happen last year when Coach Bryant won his 315th game against them.

So, I really don't have that much against Auburn players. It's Auburn fans that I can't stomach.

I don't like the way Auburn fans are laughing at us this year. And this bull about tearing down the goal posts really burns me up. Frankly I'm getting sick of hearing how this is Auburn's best chance in 10 years to beat us. Shoot, Auburn hasn't beaten Alabama since that 1972 "Punt, Bama, Punt" game, but every year it's the same thing—"We're going to beat ya'll this year." It gets old.

That doesn't mean, however, that I am not concerned. I am. And I think my friend Paul is worried, too.

"You know," Paul said yesterday, "with the way we've been breaking all the wrong records this year, I sure hope we don't screw up and lose to Auburn, too."

Don't worry, Paul ol' buddy, it's not going to happen.

The Governor is in hog heaven.

As long as I can remember, the Governor has loved telling his punters about the 1972 Auburn game—sort of a perverse reminder, I guess.

And yesterday, the Governor was at his best. He had brought a tape recording of the "Punt, Bama, Punt" game into the cafeteria at Bryant Hall and was playing the radio broadcast full blast during lunch hour.

"Alabama drops back to punt again—the punt is off—No! No! No! It's blocked! It's blocked! . . ."

You should have seen the Governor smile.

The Governor is Jack Rutledge. He's our assistant coach in charge of the kicking game. He's been called the Governor for years because I am told he looks so much like John Patterson, a former Alabama governor. But he reminds me more of comedian Don Rickles—pot-bellied, balding, and always wearing a goofy grin. I also call him Happy Jack.

He is also the one responsible for enforcing the rules in Bryant Hall, but almost everyone around here likes him anyway. He lives in the dorm with us, so it's pretty tough to sneak anything past him. When it comes to curfew violations, he can be as mean or as flexible as he wants. Usually, he's pretty reasonable.

It takes a sharp guy to keep a whole football (and basketball) team in line. It's a dirty job, but somebody's got to do it. The Governor makes bed checks, breaks up fights between room-mates, and makes certain no one is sneaking girls into his dorm room or smoking those left-handed cigarettes.

The Governor does a good job, though. And thanks to such space-age technology as the tape recorder, he's gotten the job down to an art.

You won't see the Governor walking around Bryant Hall without that darn tape recorder in his hand. He will post himself in the lobby at Bryant Hall at nights, waiting to catch anyone breaking curfew.

When someone does come in too late, the Governor will whip out the tape recorder like a gun and begin the interrogation.

"Joe Blow, it's 3 a.m., one hour past curfew," he will say. "Where have you been?"

It can get pretty hairy sometimes. So you had better make sure you have your story straight because the tape recorder is the Governor's safeguard in the event the offender tries to change his story the next day.

Depending on the seriousness of the violation and what kind of mood the Governor is in, the tape may be forwarded to Coach Bryant for further action. But if it's something the Governor feels he can handle without bothering Coach Bryant, he dishes out the punishment himself.

Even *I* have been caught. After a late date one night I thought I could sneak in past curfew. I opened the glass door as quietly as possible, and began tip-toeing toward the stairway to my room. But as I turned the corner, I saw the Governor sitting in the lobby with that darn tape recorder in his hand. He looked at me, and then at his watch. I took the hint.

"Oh, sorry I'm late, Coach," I said, as I began backing up the stairs. "I'm going. I'm going right up to my room. Right now, right this second. You don't have to worry about me, no siree."

I turned and began 4.3-ing it upstairs, halfway expecting him to call me back for an explanation. But when he didn't call me back, I got brave. Or stupid.

Once inside my room, I discovered I wasn't sleepy. So, I decided to see what Ken Coley was doing at this late hour. I stuck my head outside the door. The coast was clear. I had only taken four steps when I saw the Governor coming around the corner. I almost jumped out of my skin. Before you could say "Tuscaloosa," I was back in my room with the lights out and covers pulled over my head.

I tried to convince myself that he didn't see me. But he did.

The next morning at breakfast, he stopped by my table. I thought I was a goner until I saw him grinning from ear to ear.

"Who was that I saw sneaking around the hallway last night?" he asked with a wink.

"Uh. . .uh," I stuttered. "Not me, Coach."

"Hmm," he said, "it sure did look like you."

"Aw, must've been somebody that just looked like me," I said.

He just laughed and that was that. I never heard any more about it.

But the Governor is nobody's fool. Last year, a couple of freshmen thought they could sneak out of the dorm after curfew by using the old pillows-under-bedsheet game. The next day, the Governor had an announcement to make.

"You freshmen may like to know something," he said. "I'm smarter than I look and making those dummies in your bed has been tried before. If I see'em again, those dummies will have a better chance of making this football team than you will."

Oh well, it was worth a try.

In case you missed it, today was Thanksgiving Day. Thanksgiving is an easy holiday to miss around here because it usually occurs right around the time we are getting ready to play Auburn. Unless you are from Tuscaloosa or married and live off campus, nobody goes home for Thanksgiving because of all the team meetings we have. As a result, Thanksgiving is pretty much a non-holiday.

The coaching staff tries to make it as much fun for us as possible, though. We had a big turkey dinner down in the cafeteria. All the kitchen workers had fixed up the dining room real nice with fancy crimson-and-white napkins and stuff. Still, it wasn't like being home for the holiday.

So, I took the advice Coach Bryant gives on his South Central Bell commercial—I "called my mama" back home in Mobile and talked about two hours. That made her happy, Coach Bryant happy, and South Central Bell very, very rich.

Practicing for Auburn is serious business. You can tell that by the way the assistant coaches are acting.

They are not wasting a minute, and they crawl your butt in a hurry if you screw up. They have become perfectionists and the practices are so organized we look like the Grambling University Drill Team out there.

Coach Bryant must really be applying the pressure on the assistants to win this game. When he gets up there in his tower, every coach moves like he is walking on eggs. They all think that Coach Bryant is watching nobody but him.

Even Coach Bobby Marks, who is a pretty easy-going person, is acting that way. Just Tuesday I was standing around with some other receivers, just sort of joking around in practice when Coach Marks ran up to us.

"Damn, boys!" he said. "What are you trying to do—get me fired?"

He was only joking. . .I think.

November 26

It's started again.

Rumors are flying everywhere that Coach Bryant will retire very soon now, and that bothers me because I'm afraid they may be true this time.

The sportswriters have drawn a few conclusions about Wednesday's visit by Namath and Jordan. They think this was a case of Coach Bryant calling in the family for The Big Announcement. That sounds a little too dramatic to me.

We've gone through these rumors before, but there is something about this particular rumor that is different, something that makes me think that there really *is* something going on.

This is the first time that I've actually heard names being tossed around—names of possible candidates to follow Coach Bryant. I've heard Gene Stallings, Bobby Bowden, and Ray Perkins mentioned. I haven't heard Coach Moore's name.

I'm not sure how I feel about any of these people replacing Coach Bryant. Each has ties to Coach Bryant, each is probably a pretty good coach, and each and every one of them must be crazy as a loon to want to follow the winningest coach of all time. Any of them would probably do a good job of keeping Alabama's football tradition alive. But right now, I prefer to think of it as just another rumor. I can't imagine an Alabama football game without Coach Bryant on the sidelines.

A sportswriter friend of mine told me today that he asked Coach Bryant where he thought these latest rumors were coming from.

Coach Bryant replied, "Aw, s---! Have they started that again? Why don't you ask the Auburn Athletic Department?"

Coach Bryant's answer did not surprise me. Coach Bryant has never been much of an Auburn fan anyway. You can see that he dislikes Auburn just by looking at his eyes when he mentions their name. I can't blame him for that. Auburn has really given Coach Bryant problems the last few recruiting seasons. Everytime he moves into sign a prize prospect to a scholarship, somebody puts a bug in the kid's ear that Coach Bryant is on the verge of retiring. Before you know it, the recruit has signed with someone else.

Actually, Coach Bryant may have hurt himself when he hinted at retirement after the LSU game. That premature announcement may have scared off a half dozen top prospects. I think Coach Bryant later realized that and tried to play it down the next week.

Under the state law, Coach Bryant has to retire on his birthday next September 11. There have been some influential people trying to get the law changed with something they're calling the Bear Bryant Retirement Bill. But even if they fail, Coach Bryant could stay on and coach for free. He loves the game so much that he might just do that. I hope so anyway.

I've heard that Coach Bryant has tried to offset some of the retirement talk by having a facelift last summer—you know, a younger-looking Bryant to impress the mommas and daddys. But to tell you the truth, Coach Bryant has never looked as tired and worn out as he does now.

Just yesterday I realized how tired he must be after 38 years of coaching. When he walked into the locker room before practice, he looked as though he hadn't slept in days. His eyes were pale and watery, his hands trembled, and he sort of shuffled his feet when he walked.

When he climbs into his tower, I cringe. That tower is so high and has so many steps that I'm afraid he will fall and break his hip or something. But he has climbed those steps so often he could probably do it backwards with his eyes closed.

His speech, never the clearest in the world, has not improved with age either. His sentences are so fragmented at times that understanding him is next to impossible. That's why sportswriters are always writing, "Bryant growled" or "Bryant mumbled."

I have decided that Coach Bryant simply speaks a new language, a language that has taken me three years to understand. I know what he's saying most of the time now, but a few years ago, I just nodded, "Yes, sir" to everything he said.

I am embarrassed that I still don't know the first words Coach Bryant said to me. I had come up for my first recruiting visit, and Coach Marks carried me to Bryant Hall cafeteria to meet Coach Bryant.

"Coach Bryant," Coach Marks said, "I'd like you to meet Joey Jones from Murphy High School in Mobile."

"Humlglph?" Coach Bryant said, or something like that anyway.

I didn't know what to say—if, indeed, I was supposed to say anything. I didn't want to say, "Huh?" and sound like an idiot. So, I just sat there and smiled. He probably thought I was an idiot anyway.

I don't feel too badly about it, though. The assistant coaches have had years to learn Bryant-ese, and they still find themselves confused at times.

I remember one day at practice Coach Bryant was in his tower as usual. We were running some plays that we had just installed when suddenly we heard this loud noise. It was Coach Bryant shouting through his bull horn.

"Nawlkdkfzkk!" the noise echoed. "Nawlkdkfzkk!"

Everybody froze in their tracks. Coach Moore went berserk.

"What'd he say? What'd he say?" Mal was asking everybody around him. "Does anybody know what he said?"

Nobody knew. And nobody dared ask Coach Bryant either.

So, we did the only thing we could do—we ran the same play again. Only this time we made damn sure we got it right.

It just occurred to me that you might want to know something about Auburn's football team.

Well, Auburn is 7-3 just like us—only they are *proud* of it.

They talk about their 2-point loss to Florida, and they talk about their 5-point loss to Georgia. They do not talk about their 41-7 loss to Nebraska.

Auburn is also going to play Boston College in the Tangerine Bowl in Orlando on December 18. That's just great—we go to Memphis and freeze our butts off and they get to soak up the Florida sunshine.

Auburn has come a long way since they hired Pat Dye as their head coach. Dye's first coaching job was at Alabama, and everything he knows he learned from Coach Bryant. Dye even says so himself.

It has taken awhile for the Auburn fans to accept an ex-Alabama man as their coach. They just didn't think it was proper. But Dye began winning, and suddenly, it wasn't so bad having an Alabama man on their side. Oh well, if you can't beat 'em, join 'em.

Since Dye took over, Auburn is beginning to look more and more like Alabama. He's done away with their veer offense and gone to the wishbone. And he's hired two former Alabama players, Wayne Hall and Neil Callaway, as his assistants. The changes have picked Auburn out of the dumps, and they are now having success recruiting against us. Their most recent catch is Bo Jackson, a big halfback from Birmingham who supposedly turned down a $250,000 offer to sign with the New York Yankees.

We were in the running to sign Jackson until some unexpected turn of events. I don't know what those events were, but I do know Jackson's mother was quoted in the newspapers as saying she didn't want her son to come to Alabama because of all the drugs and racial problems here. Hmmm, I wonder who told her that?

Jackson is a good player for a freshman. Auburn fans are trying to build him up as the next Herschel Walker. Time will tell about that.

I like their other halfback better. Lionel James is fast and strong. But better than that—he's two inches shorter than I am.

Their quarterback is Randy Campbell. He's slow and probably has the weakest arm in the Southeastern Conference, but he's a competitor.

But there's no sense worrying over their offense. That's a job our defense will have to take care of. My only concern is

Auburn's defense, particularly their secondary. Luckily for me, they aren't very good, but they are getting better.

I am really looking forward to meeting David King again. King is a sophomore cornerback from Fairhope near Mobile. So, all my friends back home will rib me if he beats me on a pass play or gets the best of me. King is only an inch taller and 10 pounds heavier than I am, but he's smart. And he's fast. I worry more about those kind of players than the big guys. I'll take a 200-pound linebacker over a small but smart-and-fast player any day. You can beat those big players because they're usually so slow. Besides, they don't hurt you half as much as it may look.

King is the kind of player you really have to watch. He's a big play man, the kind of player who will rush in and block a kick or cause you to fumble.

King *does* make mistakes, however. I've noticed on game films that he sometimes plays too close to the line of scrimmage. When a defensive back gets six or seven yards from me, I start smiling because I know I can beat them. They will be running backwards while I'll be moving full speed ahead.

One quick note before the bus leaves for Birmingham: Coach Marks says Auburn has the best defensive backfield we've seen all year. We'll see about that tomorrow. . .

November 28.

Forget what I said about not hating Auburn. I have changed my mind.

I *do* hate them.

In fact, I despise them.

Yes, we lost. Auburn beat us 23-22. And yes, they tore down the damn goal post. I hope they choke on it.

I don't know how Paul is feeling today. I slept until 2 o'clock and he was nowhere in sight when I awakened. Paul got a bad cut on his chin during the game, so he's probably at the training room getting that checked out. He was right about us breaking another record, you know. Now we'll hear about "23-22" for the next 10 years.

I purposely slept through Coach Bryant's TV show. I don't

think I could stand to watch it all again—too embarrasing.

I keep telling myself that I'm not to blame. I caught three passes for 64 yards, scored the game's first touchdown, I whipped David King all over the field, and I even threw the block on King that sprung Paul for his touchdown.

I could talk about the statistics, I guess:

First Downs—Us 27, Them 11.

Yards Rushing—Us 256, Them 193.

Yards Passing—Us 251, Them 64.

Passing—Us 18 of 33 with 2 interceptions, Them 6 of 14, no interceptions.

Statistically speaking, we kicked their tail. But statistics don't mean a thing when you lose. Auburn beat us where it counted—on the scoreboard.

Maybe, what we need is a new statistic, something to reflect the variables that do not show up on the scoreboard. I would like to suggest "TDs-ABQC," for Touchdowns Aided By Questionable Calls." Auburn got its share of those. I don't mean to sound like a sore loser, but losing makes me grouchy. Besides, our team rule (Show Your Class, Not Your Ass) forbids us from saying anything negative about an opponent or officiating. I just hope that crew of officials went to church today.

In the meantime, I'll let the facts speak for themselves.

We had run only six offensive plays before I realized the breaks would not be going our way. We had a third down at Auburn's 37-yard-line, and I had just caught one of my special belly-busters along the sideline. Only the official ruled that I was out of bounds—I wasn't. We argued the call and ended up getting hit with a delay of game penalty. The drive died and we punted.

Auburn pulled one of the stupidest moves I've ever seen in college football on its next possession. Facing a fourth down with a yard to go from their own 48, they sent Greg Pratt, a backup fullback, over left guard. Jackie Cline and Mike Pitts politely rearranged his head and we took over.

Walter picked up four yards on a keeper around left end to give us a second-and-six at the Auburn 45. Things were looking good, but Walter was looking nervous. In the huddle, Walter called for a reverse to Jesse's side but then changed it to my side. As I went back to the line I wondered if Walter had his plays straight. He did. I got 13 yards on the reverse and a first down at

Auburn's 32. A few plays later, Walter found me open in the end zone for a 22-yard touchdown pass. And with Peter Kim's extra point kick, we took a 7-0 lead with 4:44 left in the left in the first quarter.

Auburn couldn't get anything going and punted again. On our first play, I gained 15 yards on a pass from Walter and I must have embarrassed Auburn's defensive back, Tim Drinkard, by catching it. After he tackled me, he punched me in the ribs as he was getting up. That was when I decided I didn't like Auburn any more. Before long, we were at Auburn's 28. But then, Joe Carter fumbled the ball and Drinkard picked it up and carried it 60 yards to our 19 before Walter pulled him down. But I wasn't worried— not then, and not even three plays later when they tied up the score.

It took us two more series before we scored again: a field goal by Peter. We were ahead again, 10-7.

We had started another drive when Bob Harris picked off Walter's pass to Jeff Fagan. Auburn got the ball at our 24. It didn't take long before Randy Campbell went two yards over right tackle for the touchdown. Al Del Greco kicked the conversion and Auburn led, 14-10.

Ken Coley took over for Walter at quarterback on the final drive of the half and carried us 65 yards to Auburn's 15. We had a first down, but only a few seconds left, so Peter kicked a 33-yard field goal. We went into halftime trailing 14-13.

In the dressing room, Coach Bryant was calm. "We have earned everything we've gotten today," Coach Bryant said. "Auburn hasn't earned anything. Every point they have has been given to them. We've got to cut out the mistakes, the turnovers. Other than that, you are doing a good job. Keep up the good work." Coach Bryant was right. We knew we were a better team, and we were determined to prove it in the second half.

After Paul returned the second-half kickoff 31 yards, it wasn't long before we had the ball at Auburn's 8-yard line. On the next play, Paul took the pitch from Walter and headed around right end. I cut down the last defender, David King, and Paul carried it in for the touchdown. We needed a two-point conversion, but Paul couldn't hold on to Walter's pass and the score stayed at 19-14, our favor.

Peter gave us another field goal before the third quarter was over, and we seemed to be in good shape with a 22-14 lead. But Bo Jackson broke through left tackle with a 53-yard run and Auburn got a 23-yard field goal to cut it to 22-17.

It was still that way with just over three minutes left in the game. Auburn had the ball and was driving. They were at our 46 when Campbell threw a 16-yard pass across the middle to Chris Woods. Two plays later, Campbell threw to Woods again, but Jeremiah Castille cut across and intercepted. I thought we were home free. That was when I saw the ref come running from the far side of the field to throw a penalty flag toward Jeremiah.

"Pass interference," he said.

"Like hell it is!" Jeremiah said.

Jeremiah had played the ball, not the receiver, but had brushed him on the interception. It was a judgment call at best. We were penalized 21 yards and Auburn had a first down at our 9-yard line. Time was running out. Three more plays and they had a fourth-and-goal from our 1-yard line.

The stadium was going crazy. There was so much noise you could hardly hear yourself think, but Coach Ken Donahue was thinking. He figured Jackson would get the ball and he was right. So, when Campbell handed the ball to Jackson, we had bodies stacked 10-feet high on the goal line. I thought Jackson would have needed wings to get over that pile. His feet left the ground two steps from the goal line, and I held my breath for what seemed to be an eternity. When the ref blew the play dead and I saw Mike Pitts, Stan Gay and Tommy Wilcox celebrating, I knew we had held them.

But I was wrong. The ref was signaling a touchdown. And Auburn had it's "TD ABQC."

Our luck and time was running out. Two minutes, 26 seconds was plenty of time for us to kick a field goal, and Auburn didn't want to take that chance. So, they went for the two-point conversion and blew it.

We blew it, too. All we needed was a field goal, but Walter was intercepted again and Auburn ran out the clock. End of game, end of streak, end of season.

I didn't hang around for the celebration. The fans were climbing over the fences before I got off the field. I could still hear the "War Damn Eagle" screams from inside the locker room. The dressing room was like a morgue.

"You don't have anything to be ashamed of," Coach Bryant said. "You played a good game, probably the best game you've played all season. It just wasn't enough."

My mother, aunt and uncle were waiting for me outside the locker room. They tried their best to avoid talking about the game. They wanted me to go to dinner with them. But I was in no mood for food—what I needed was a cold beer. So I declined Mom's invitation, kissed her good-bye, and joined Scott McRae, Mike Rodriguez, Richard Shinn and a few other of the guys at the Ramada Inn. We had already paid a deposit for a couple of rooms there. It was supposed to be our victory party, but it wasn't much of a party at all. I drowned my sorrows until 1:30 a.m. and then headed back to Tuscaloosa.

Suddenly, I dreaded the Liberty Bowl more than ever.

PART III

Say It Ain't So

November 29, 1982
Bryant Hall

I'm feeling almost human again.

We have a few days off before we begin practice for the Liberty Bowl and I hardly know how to behave with all this free time. It's shocking to find that there is a whole other world outside Bryant Hall.

I guess that's my biggest complaint about college football—playing time. Not the kind on the field, but the kind off of it. A player's time is so regimented during the season that there is hardly time for anything except football. If you're not in the classroom, you're in a team meeting. Or practicing. Or lifting weights. Or watching game films. Or studying for an exam. And that plays heck on your social life.

But once there is a break in the schedule and that curfew comes down, watch out. Tuscaloosa isn't safe from anyone. Even mild-mannered people like Jim Ivy can become a holy terror.

Ivy is a big offensive tackle from Birmingham who looks a lot like Elvis Presley after Elvis got fat. But he's really a nice guy and he keeps everybody loose by mocking Steve Booker's gosh-awful habit of saying, "No, man, looky here." Ivy's never had a cross word for anyone except maybe Peter Kim. But Peter knows Tae Kwon Do and when he told Ivy, "Shut up, you big fat country boy," Ivy laughed. But he shut up.

Anyway, to get back to the story, Ivy went out with some guys one night and bent his elbow one too many times at the bar. In Ivy's case, that means he might have drunk as many as two beers. Even that is too much for Ivy. So around 2 a.m., Bryant Hall came alive with the sound of Ivy.

"Arruuugh! Arruuugh!"

It sounded like a rabid bear in heat.

"Arruuugh! Arruuugh!"

Finally, our curiosity got the best of us. Just like a fire drill, every door to every room on the second floor swung open. We all wanted to see what kind of animal made such a noise. The animal was Ivy, his head and shoulders buried to his waist in a garbage can and barfing his brains out. When he realized he had attracted a rather large audience, Ivy pulled up from the trash can, looked around at us and said, "No, man, don't look at me! You looky here!"

Sammy Hood, a defensive back from Ider, is another one who has trouble holding his liquor. But unlike Ivy, Sammy sometimes get violent. Sammy falls somewhere between the good ol' boy you see on *Dukes of Hazzard* and the kind of guy who spends Saturday nights circling the local Dairy King looking for a fight. He drives an old beat up Plymouth Duster that is painted like the *Starsky and Hutch* car and jacked up in the rear end. And Sammy does love a good fight.

So, one night after a night out at a local drinking establishment, Sammy met Wes Neighbors in the parking lot, and before you know it they were tearing into each other like two alley cats. Paul and I had just driven up in the nick of time and proceeded to break it up. But Sammy had his country pride and wasn't about to back down. Paul and I somehow managed to pry Sammy away and forcefully carried him back to the dorm. We thought we had him calmed down and sobered up, but as soon as Wes showed up, Sammy started in again. Sammy doesn't know when to quit.

Now that I've spoiled the myth that football players never drink anything stronger than Gatorade, perhaps I should stress that there is *not* a drinking problem here. Drinking is something that is done only as a sideline while looking for girls. Girls, on the other hand *are* a problem. There doesn't seem to be enough of them.

Contrary to popular belief, football players are not seduced in every town where we play. We are not pursued by every beauty queen on campus. And cheerleaders and majorettes are not "sure things" for us. You can't just walk into a bar and say, "Hi, I'm an

Alabama football player" and dozens of girls will want to take you home to perform unnatural acts over your body. Yes, kiddies, even an Alabama football player can end up without a date to the prom.

Oh, there are exceptions. There are tales of one well-known quarterback (who shall remain nameless) who lured girls to Thomas Field late at night and made love to them in the moonlight in Coach Bryant's tower. "It's a thrill they'll never forget," he said. I'm sure. Then, there are the groupie types who hang around a team hotel on road trips, trying to pick up players. But those are not the kind of girls you want to take home to Mom.

Of course, any time you start talking about girls with a teammate, you have to use your own judgement on what is fact and what is fiction. Even then, you must consider the source. Which brings me to Perry Cuda . . .

Perry is a sophomore quarterback and a real ladies' man. Unlike most sane people, he once turned down Brooke Shields.

It all began when Perry was being recruited by one of the West Coast schools, UCLA or Southern Cal. Some rich alumnus apparently used his influence to have Brooke meet Perry and try to sweet talk him into signing. Perry, like a dummy, did not. And even after he signed with Alabama, he got a call from Brooke asking him to attend a banquet of some kind in Los Angeles or somewhere. But that invitation came during the season, and Perry again declined. Now that's dedication!

Ken Coley is another lady killer quarterback. He gets his girls with his blue eyes, blond hair and Pepsodent smile. Roosevelt Hill, a linebacker from Newman, Georgia, brags about keeping four women on a string at once just by smooth-talking them. Jerrill Sprinkle, a defensive back who comes from a wealthy family in Atlanta, can flash his perfect teeth and win just about any girl's heart.

Me? I'm not a looker or a talker, so I try to compensate with humor. Lucky for me, it works. One night at a local night club, I cut in front of a friend and began dancing and clowning around with his girl. I must have really been funny that night because my friend didn't break my legs and the girl didn't slap my face.

The girl is Elise Lapeyre, a graphic design student at

Alabama. She came to Alabama on a volleyball scholarship, and when the volleyball program was dropped, she tried to get me to talk Coach Bryant into reinstating it. I can just see myself asking Coach Bryant to bring back volleyball. Love is blind, but it doesn't make you stupid...

December 2.

The fun is over. It's back to work.

Practice started for the Liberty Bowl today and it was a disaster. The offensive line wasn't blocking, the defensive line wasn't tackling, the running backs were moving in slow motion, and the receivers weren't receiving—myself included.

The problem is the game itself. Nobody gives a darn about the Liberty Bowl, and we care even less about spending the Christmas holidays in Memphis. I've seen all those pictures of the 1976 Liberty Bowl game against UCLA when Coach Bryant was bundled up like a cold-natured Eskimo. It makes my bones ache just to think about it. I hate cold weather—it makes me appreciate living in Mobile. It does not make me appreciate Bowl games.

But Bowl games are a necessary evil, I guess. They make the university richer and in a round-about way help determine a national champion. Since we are not playing for a national championship, I can only assume we are playing to raise money for the swim team.

Bowl games have become a joke. There are so many of them that just about everybody goes to a bowl after the regular season. And if you're not good enough to get into one of the existing bowls, there always seems to be another rinky-dink town out there willing to hold a bowl game just for you. More than half of the Southeastern Conference got bowl bids this year. Georgia meets Penn State in the Sugar Bowl, LSU meets Nebraska in the Orange Bowl, Florida meets Arkansas in the Bluebonnet, Tennessee meets Iowa in the Peach, Auburn has Boston College in the Tangerine, Vanderbilt meets Air Force in the Hall of Fame, and, of course, we've got Illinois in the Liberty.

Idealistically, a bowl game is supposed to be a reward for the players. Idealistically, it's a week-long vacation in a resort city such as New Orleans, Miami, Los Angeles or Dallas. Players are fed exotic dinners, loaded down with watches or other gifts and souvenirs, pampered by voluptuous bowl "hostesses," and get to paint the town red at night.

But realistically, it's another story. A lot depends on where you are. And if you're not in the Orange, Rose, Sugar or Gator bowls, then your chances of having a good time are pretty slim. So, depending on which bowl invitation you receive, a bowl can either be a punishment or reward. And I think we are being punished.

When Coach Bryant called in all the seniors to decide which bowl invitation we would accept, he told them that we deserve a bowl invitation this year. Then, he gave the seniors three choices: (1) accept the Liberty Bowl bid, (2) wait for a Fiesta Bowl bid that may not come, or (3) play in the Hall of Fame Bowl in Birmingham. Don't laugh—that last choice was all Coach Bryant's idea. He told the seniors that if we were determined to go to a bowl game, then we should do something good for the State of Alabama by playing in the Hall of Fame. He said that by playing in Birmingham, we would be keeping money in the state and be giving people jobs. Of course, it was an honorable idea, but it went over like a lead balloon with the seniors. Ken Coley was really upset about it. I remember he came back from the meeting in a near state of shock.

"I can't believe it! I just can't believe it!" Ken said to me.

"Believe what?" I asked. "What did he say?"

"He wanted us to go to the Hall of Shame Bowl!" Ken screamed. "Can you believe that—the Hall of Shame Bowl!"

I couldn't blame Ken for feeling that way. He's from Birmingham so that would be no trip at all for him, especially since we've become used to the Sugar Bowl.

So, the seniors really had only two choices—give us Liberty or give us Fame. The Hall of Fame was rejected unanimously. And now, we've got the Liberty, but I don't believe our hearts are in it.

December 7

Lot of individual awards coming out these days. First there was the Heisman, then the Associated Press All-SEC teams, and today came the AP All-American team.

Guess what? I didn't make any of them.

That's why I envy Mike Pitts and Jeremiah Castille. Both were named second team on the AP All-American today, and both deserve it. Jeremiah is one of our team leaders and about as dedicated as you can get. He's one of the best defensive backs we've ever had. No matter how many fakes I put on him, no matter how many quick moves I make, Jeremiah is always there. Pitts, on the other hand, leads by example. He's the big, silent type who eats quarterbacks for breakfast.

Jeremiah and Mike also made first team All-SEC along with Joe Beazley, an offensive tackle. Steve Mott, our "warped" game captain, made second team All-SEC along with our resident cajun, Tommy Wilcox.

Sure, it bothers me that I didn't make *any* of these all-star teams but that's about all I can expect as long as we run the wishbone. Besides, individual awards don't mean much if the team doesn't do well. . .

December 10.

I wonder if a team has ever failed to show up for a bowl game?

If not, I'd say we've got an excellent chance of breaking that record, too. The seniors are regretting their vote for a bowl game. This is one game we could all do without.

I was right about our hearts not being in this one. You can tell by the way practice has been going. Oh, I know it's hard to get excited about playing a team such as Illinois, especially with exams going on and Christmas coming up. But our practices aren't just bad—they're awful. When the ball is snapped, it's a Mexican standoff between the offensive and defensive lines. Nobody wants to make the first move.

We are a team without a motive—without a cause. What do we have to gain? Certainly not a national championship. And if we lose? Heaven knows we could kiss the Top 20 goodbye.

We've got 19 days to come up with a miracle—Broadway Joe, are you listening?

December 15.

Where do you begin on a day such as this? I don't know

how to begin, where to start. I'm sure you know why.

Coach Bryant announced his retirement today. I guess you've already heard about it—everybody else has. It was all over the TV and radio. In a way, it's almost funny—it's just that I never thought it would happen like this. I always thought it would be like a gigantic family reunion—Coach Bryant would tell all of us about it two weeks before he made it public and we'd throw a huge retirement party for him at Bryant-Denny. But it just didn't happen that way. None of us were expecting it.

Initially, I guess you could say I was shocked. After that, I began to feel guilty, guilty that I didn't take some very important advice he gave us time and time again.

"Take time to stop and think every day," he was always telling us. "Take stock of what is happening around you and you will understand it better. Don't wait until it's too late. Don't wait until something drastic happens before you sit down and think things over."

I couldn't count how many times I've heard him say that. . . I guess I wasn't listening. And now, something drastic *has* happened.

I'm so confused—I've gone from feeling betrayed to feeling angry to feeling selfish and sad. But most of all, I feel guilty, I guess. I keep thinking that if we had won just two more games Coach Bryant wouldn't be retiring January 1, and I wouldn't be so worried about what kind of coach Ray Perkins will be. If we had just tried a *little* harder, just given a *little* more—maybe he wouldn't. . . .

Maybe I am wrong to draw these conclusions without first hearing what Coach Bryant has to say. But I haven't had the chance because I missed *the* meeting—the most important meeting of my life and I missed it. I'll never get over that.

It all started last night around 10 o'clock. The Governor had given me permission to break curfew in order to study for a math test with Joe Morgan, a friend of mine from Mobile, at Joe's house. Joe and I had the television tuned to the local cable channel and were studying while watching the Automated News Network. I wasn't paying much attention to the TV when Joe punched me on the shoulder.

"Look!" he said, pointing to the television.

That's when I saw the first bulletin on the screen. I don't

remember exactly what it said, only that Coach Bryant was expected to resign Wednesday and be replaced by Ray Perkins, coach of the National Football League's New York Giants.

"Do you think it's true?" Joe asked.

"Naw, can't be," I answered confidently. "He would have told us first."

I turned back to the television.

The reports continued. Rumors had been circulating throughout the day, it said. And there were press conferences supposedly scheduled for Wednesday in Tuscaloosa and at Giants Stadium in East Rutherford, New Jersey. The words "rumors" and "reportedly" were used several times.

"See?" I told Joe. "They are still using words like 'rumors' and 'reportedly.' That's all it is—just another rumor."

Joe was convinced, but deep down, I began to wonder. Could it really be true? Could Coach Bryant be retiring? And if he was, why had I not heard of any meeting? Coach Bryant wouldn't take such a big step without first talking to the team. Would he? I just didn't know.

My concentration for the rest of the night was ruined. But I tried to study for several more hours before finally falling asleep on Joe's sofa.

When I woke up around 7:30 this morning, the TV was still on. And reports of Coach Bryant retiring were still moving accusingly across the screen. Only this time, the reports sounded more definite. There was even a report about a meeting he was supposed to have had with the players. That did it. I decided I had to find out what was going on. I telephoned Paul back at the dorm.

"Paul," I said, "I keep hearing all this stuff about Coach Bryant retiring. Have you heard anything?"

"I'm afraid it's true, Joey," Paul said. His voice sounded weak, shaky. I knew he was upset.

"He *is* retiring," Paul went on. "We had a team meeting with him just a few minutes ago."

"Damn!" I said. "Why didn't you call me?"

"Didn't have time," he said apologizing. "Besides, I didn't know how to get in touch with you."

"Damn!" I said again. "I can't believe I missed it, a meeting *that* important—I just can't believe I missed it."

I suddenly regretted studying. There would be other math tests, but there would never ever be another meeting like that one.

"What did he say?" I finally asked.

"Nothing much," Paul replied.

"What do you mean, 'nothing much?'" I insisted. "He must have said *something.*"

"Well—yes, but he didn't make a big deal out of it," Paul said. "He just called us all in and said that it was time for him to retire. It was real casual, about like announcing that he was going to stop by the grocery store after practice. The meeting didn't last long, just about two minutes."

Two minutes? I couldn't believe it. The man spends 38 years of his life coaching, and ends it all in just two short minutes? No long goodbyes? No teary farewells?

I had more questions but I could see Paul was in no mood for giving answers. Besides, I still had to get to class and take that dang math test.

So while I was sitting in class, Coach Bryant was announcing his retirement to the press. I did manage to get a transcript of his retirement speech. Here it is:

> There comes a time in every profession when you need to hang it up and that time has come for me as head football coach at the University of Alabama.
>
> My main purpose as Director of Athletics and head football coach here at Alabama has been to field the best possible teams, to improve each player as a person and to produce citizens who will be a credit to our present-day society.
>
> We have been successful in most of those areas, but now, I feel the time is right for a change in our football leadership. We lost two big games this season that we should have won, and we played only four or five games like Bryant-coached teams should play. I've done a poor job of coaching.
>
> This is my school—my alma mater—and I love it. And I love the players—but in my opinion, they deserve better coaching than

they've been getting from me this year and my stepping down is an effort to see that they get better coaching from someone else.

It is a great joy for me, personally, to have had the opportunity to coach at my alma mater. I know I will miss coaching, but the thing I will miss most is the association I have had with the players, the coaches, the competition—all of those things that have made such a strong tradition at Alabama.

I can't say enough, or thank enough, the coaches who are with me now—and those who have been there in the past.

I plan to continue as Director of Athletics and pledge my support to my successor in every respect, particularly in recruiting. . .

That was about it. By the time the press conference ended, I had my exam and it was time for practice—one of the strangest practices I've ever been through. It was raining so we had moved into the Coliseum. I was halfway expecting a long speech, a goodbye speech or something, but Coach Bryant just came in, cracked a joke and left in just a few minutes. Jimmy Watts, a linebacker, said, "God, he's acting like nothing has happened." He was right. And when he left the gym, a wave of emptiness filled the room. Hardly anyone said a word—didn't have to. I didn't think practice could get any worse than the ones we had been having, but this one was. The Liberty Bowl was the farthest thing from anybody's mind.

Bryant Hall was a madhouse after practice. The lobby downstairs was filled with newspaper and television reporters. As soon as a player walked in, some reporter would grab him by the arm and start asking questions.

"Joey, what do you think about Coach Bryant retiring?" they would ask.

Or, "Joey how do you feel about Ray Perkins as your new coach?"

Or, "Joey, are you glad to see the pro style offense coming in?"

The same questions over and over and over. How was *I* supposed to know how I felt or what to expect? The reporters knew as much as I did. After all, they had talked to Coach Bryant—I hadn't. I put up with their questions as long as I could and then excused myself. I ran upstairs to my room. I wanted to be alone to sort things out.

But I wasn't alone. Dante Bramblett was there with Paul and they were already talking about everything that had happened.

"Those damn reporters!" I said, clenching my teeth as I closed the door behind me.

"Yeah, I know," said Paul, looking up. "They're everywhere. I can't believe the nerve of some of those guys."

"Well, Joey," Dante said, "why do you think Coach Bryant's retiring? You think he's lost his magic touch like he says he has?

"No," I said, "That's not it. He knows he's the best there is. He's just too modest to admit it. I think it's because of recruiting. You know how all those retirement rumors have affected recruiting. Nobody wants to come in here and get caught in the transition. Everybody wants to spend all four years playing for The Bear."

"You're right there," Paul agreed. "I know I thought he would always be here. I thought I'd be spending all four years under him."

"Me, too," said Dante. "He's the reason I came here."

"He's the reason we *all* came here," I said. "But that's all beside the point now. Now, we are caught in the middle—damn! I hope Perkins doesn't come in and start changing everything around like a lot of new coaches do. I don't want to spend my last year here rebuilding. I want to win a national championship before I leave this place, not start all over again."

"I know what you mean," said Paul. "But now we've got to get used to a new coach. And we'll probably have to get used to a whole new offense, too."

"Think so?" I asked.

"Probably," Paul said. "I'll bet Perkins does away with the wishbone and goes to some pro-style like the Giants are running—you should like that, huh, Joey—catching 30 passes a game?

"I should," I said, "but I'd rather have Coach Bryant than a new offense any day. It took me forever to prove to him that I could play, and I don't want to have to prove it all over again for Perkins."

"You might have to," Dante said. "With the kind of season we have had, I'll bet Perkins fires all of the offensive coaches. I'll bet the defensive coaches stay, but not the offensive staff."

"You're probably right," Paul said.

"Well, whatever happens, I hope Coach Marks doesn't lose his job," I said. "I really like him. I don't want somebody else coming in and coaching the receivers."

"I wouldn't count on it," said Dante. "I'll betcha Perkins cleans house. He just seems like the type."

"Whaddaya mean?" I asked. "Do you know anything about him except that he played at Alabama?"

"I've seen pictures of him and I've seen him on TV," said Dante, shrugging his shoulders. "That's about all."

"But what do you mean, 'he *seems* like the type?'" I asked.

"It's just that every time I've seen a picture of him he's wearing a sneer and a three-piece suit," said Dante. "He just looks like he would be a real hard-ass, a regular Wall Street type. Maybe, I'm wrong; I hope so anyway."

"I do too," I said. "But really, as far as coaches go, he's probably a pretty good choice, don't you think? The Giants *are* in the play-offs and he *did* play here. He should have some idea of how we're used to doing things."

"Maybe so," Dante admitted, "but he's got a lot to prove—not just to us but to the fans and alumni, too. You don't follow somebody like Coach Bryant and expect to get the same reception. Coach Bryant earned his reputation the hard way, and Perkins will have to do the same."

This went on for about two hours. We sat there like prisoners on death row, guessing what was going to happen to us. And we came to a few conclusions: We are going to miss Coach Bryant; we are glad he will stay on as athletic director; and we are *not* ready to accept Ray Perkins as our new coach. In fact, if Perkins had walked into that room right then, we probably would have cussed him out on the spot.

I was still upset when I drove out to Lake Nicol late this afternoon. Lake Nicol is a park just outside Tuscaloosa where a lot of students go to study. But it was deserted today so I had it all to myself. I climbed up a steep ledge, sat down on a big rock, and cried my eyes out.

Nothing mattered any more. Losing three straight games was nothing compared to losing Coach Bryant. I was angry. I felt like Coach Bryant was running out on us. But then I realized that he was not a quitter. He wouldn't quit unless there was a good reason. I know he's worried about the football program's future, but it may be more than that. I'm afraid he's worried about his health, too. If something *is* wrong with him, if he *is* sick, it would be selfish to want him to go on, to continue coaching.

How—how do I explain it? Coach Bryant means so much to me, to everybody. With him, it's not like a coach talking down to a player—all take and no give. It's—well, he's—he's like a grandfather or a friend, so caring, understanding—the way he always stops to shake hands or talk with handicapped people in wheelchairs—I've seen him do that a thousand times.

He's still tough as nails. I've seen him cuss up a blue streak on the football field, but you always know he's doing it for your own good. I've never said he was a saint, no matter what they say about him walking on water. He says he doesn't treat everyone alike, he just treats them fairly. And he does, too. He is always saying, "If you've ever got any problems, you always come to me first. I don't care what it is—family problems, school, drugs—anything, you come to me because we can dang sure work it out."

Of course, I've never gone to him with anything. I never thought any of my problems were big enough to bother him with them. But if they were, I'm sure he'd be glad to help. I imagine everybody on the team is the same way. Maybe some players have gone to him with problems before; some may even visit him now. But if they do, you never hear about it. That's the way he kept it.

When I first came here, I thought he didn't like me because I was so small. I was always checking the sports pages and watching the *Bear Bryant Show* to see if he would mention my name. I saw or heard nothing. I wasn't getting any playing time to speak of and I thought Coach Bryant was scared I would be hurt if he put me into a game. Then I heard through the grapevine that Coach Bryant said that I "would never make it."

"Too small," he had said.

I became so depressed that I was ready to transfer to Florida

State, and I told Coach Marks of my plans.

"No, you don't want to do that little buddy," Coach Marks said. "You just stick around. You'll play here, you'll see. If I have anything to do with it, you'll play."

So I stayed, worked hard on running my routes, and even stayed after practices to improve my catches. Finally, things began to change my sophomore year. I ran a punt back in the season-opener against LSU on national television and Coach Bryant noticed. He sat next to Paul on the plane trip back to Tuscaloosa, and Paul told me later that Coach Bryant said that I had put the icing on the game. That made me feel better and restored my confidence. I began working like a madman. The next week, both Keith Marks and Jesse were hurt and I got my first start against Georgia Tech. I scored a touchdown, but we lost in an upset. I heard Coach Bryant say something like I was "doing well for a little guy." That burned me up. I was more determined than ever to show him that I was good—period, no matter what my size. Two weeks later against Vanderbilt, I caught an 81-yard pass and ran back a few long punts. I could hardly wait until Sunday to hear what Coach Bryant had to say about me on his TV show now. He didn't disappoint me.

"Yeah," Coach Bryant said, "little big man has really been working hard. He's been staying after practice and doing his best to improve. He's doing so well that I'm going to give him tomorrow off."

I nearly fell out of my chair. I really didn't think he was serious until I showed up for practice on Monday. I had stopped in front of my locker and was getting out my equipment when Coach Marks walked up and told me to put it back. "You're not practicing today," he said. "Coach Bryant's orders. You have officially gone from the outhouse to the penthouse."

I wanted to be noticed, but not like that. That much flattery was embarrassing. I didn't want to take the day off because I knew all the other players would rag me about it. But Walter Lewis told me to relax and enjoy it.

"Take it in stride," Walter said. So I did.

But from that day on, I have always been "Little Big Man" to Coach Bryant.

I honestly believe Coach Bryant knew what he was doing all along by dropping those hints about me not being able to make it here. I think he knew what I could do and was just giving me a reason to fight back. I can't thank him enough for that.

I'm sure going to miss him. . .

PART IV

This One's For You

December, 16, 1982
Bryant Hall

I woke up this morning thinking I had been dreaming. I hadn't been. Coach Bryant's retirement is still front page news.

I laid in bed for a long time, trying to decide whether to go back to sleep or get up and go to class. The intellectual side of me finally prevailed, but just barely. I hate early morning classes during the winter term. I hate crawling out of a warm bed and stepping onto cold tile floors. I hate waking through drafty hallways in my BVDs to a communal shower where hot water is a rare luxury. And I hate rushing to class with my hair still wet and cold wind whipping my face. But most of all, I hate class itself. Especially today. Today, I was simply not in the mood for getting educated, and I guess my lack of enthusiasm was showing. One teacher stared at me with sad, mournful eyes for about three minutes and then called me aside. "Look," he said, "I know how you must feel, what with Coach Bryant retiring and all—if you want to take today off, go right ahead. I won't mind." But I stayed because I thought it would take my mind off everything else. Guess what? It didn't.

I got really ticked off today. As I was walking to class, one guy who I really don't know that well came up to me and said, "You guys had better not blow this game. You just can't let Coach Bryant go out a loser."

I don't know why that made me angry, but it did. I guess it was because he made it sound like an order. But it could be because I know he's right. We *have* to win the Liberty Bowl game for him now. And that scares me.

Whomever said "practice makes perfect" hasn't seen us practice the past two days.

Today, Coach Bryant stood in his tower still acting as if nothing unusual has happened. He did not mention his retirement even once. But down on the field, progress had come to a standstill. The assistant coaches are really depressed, especially Coach Moore. He has to be upset about not being named head coach after working under Coach Bryant for so long.

Coach Moore is one of the more serious coaches on the staff. He doesn't cut up or crack jokes or anything when he's on that practice field. With him, it's all work, work, work, But today, he was unusually quiet—and unusually patient.

"Let's see. . .," he'd say in a voice so soft it was almost like he was daydreaming, ". . .let's run this play over here—no, no, let's run this play over there." Or something like that. And when we'd screw up, all he'd say was, "Oh well, that's okay. Come back and let's try it again—and try to get it right this time, OK?"

Two weeks ago, if we had made the same mistake he would have gone bonkers and screamed, "Lorrrd, have mercy!"

The really strange thing is that Coach Bryant is putting up with all this. He stands up in that tower watching us foul up and he isn't raising that much hell about it. I guess he knows our minds just aren't on the business at hand.

I'm worried about Coach Marks. As I was walking off the field today, I noticed him headed toward the tunnel that leads to the dressing room. He looked tired, almost dejected.

I yelled for him to wait up. "Hey, Coach Marks! Got a second?"

"Why sure, little man," he said. He smiled and put his arm around my shoulder and we walked on toward the dressing room. "What's on your mind?"

"I was wondering. . .," I stuttered, ". . .wondering if you've heard anything. Will you be staying on?"

Coach Marks has the kind of droopy eyes that always look sad. But at that instant, they looked even sadder, and I thought for a second that he was crying.

"I don't know, Joey," he said, shaking his head. "I haven't heard anything. I just don't know.

"I've got an interview with Perkins when he comes in next

week," he went on. "But right now, things don't look too good. I hope I get to stay. I don't want to leave this place."

"I hope so, too, Coach," I said. "I don't want you to leave either."

"Thanks, Joey," he said. He smiled weakly, patted me on the back, and disappeared into the coaches' dressing room. I felt sick to my stomach.

At least Ray Perkins knows his place. And it's behind Coach Bryant—way behind.

I got my first glimpse of our new coach today on TV. I was not overly impressed. Dante was right about him. Because there, in living color on Mike and Doug's 21-inch TV screen, was Ray Perkins, wearing a drab three-piece suit and a sneer that would make Atilla the Hun cower.

It was film footage of his press conference yesterday at Giants Stadium. He was telling the New York press why he had accepted the head coaching job here. But he made it sound so formal, so business-like that he might as well have been quoting the Dow Jones 30 industrials.

But I will say one thing for the man, he knows he has a tough act to follow, and he's doing it by trying to sound tough himself.

"I'm following—repeat, following—the greatest coach in college football," Perkins was saying. "It's a great honor to go there. If I was scared or intimidated, I wouldn't take the job. . .

"I admire him [Coach Bryant], yes; love him, yes; but intimidated by him, no."

My God, he's cocky too.

December 17

Looks like Ray Perkins has lined up some heavyweights on his side. The votes of confidence are beginning to trickle in.

I was reading where Ken Stabler, an old Tide quarterback himself (and I mean *old*) said that he thought Perkins would be "successful—if he's given time to establish himself."

I think Ken has forgotten it doesn't work that way here. Here, he should establish himself first and then we'll talk "time."

I also noticed that Jeff Rutledge and Curtis McGriff have

endorsed Perkins. They are other ex-Alabama players who are now playing for Perkins.

McGriff said, "I think it's a good move."

And Rutledge said, "The players will like him. He's fair."

Sounds great, Jeff, but if it's OK with you, I'll wait until Monday and see for myself.

I was telling Darryl White about the conversation I had with Coach Marks yesterday. He's really upset about it. He also suggested that all the receivers chip in and buy Coach Marks some kind of gift to show our appreciation in case he does get fired. So we got all the other receivers together and kicked around ideas of what we could buy him. One idea we had was a plaque of some kind with all the receivers' names engraved on it. But we discarded that idea because that's too much like giving somebody an autographed picture of yourself. We decided that since he jogs a lot, we would buy him a walkman stereo headphone. Darryl volunteered to go shopping for it.

Checked my mail today and found eight letters, one $36 phone bill, and one reminder that my car payment is past due. Of the eight letters received, five were from friends back home asking that I get Coach Bryant's autograph for them. Three even sent 8-by-10 glossy pictures to be signed. I guess I'll have to get that done when Coach Bryant isn't so busy. Come to think of it, I wouldn't mind having his autograph myself.

Oh, that reminds me—if you have something autographed by Coach Bryant, look again. The autograph you may be seeing may not be Coach Bryant's at all—it could belong to Willie Meadows, our equipment manager. In fact, I'd guess that 8 out of 10 Bear Bryant autographs floating around America today were written by none other than Willie Meadows.

Willie is an ex-Army supply officer whose job is to make certain our uniforms don't wind up in Nashville on the day we're supposed to be playing in Knoxville. But Willie's real specialty is signing Coach Bryant's signature on footballs, photographs, game programs and any other 'Bama souvenirs sent through the mail. There are just so many requests, especially these days, that I presume Coach Bryant asked Willie to grab a pen and help out. And why not? He can sign Coach Bryant's name better than Coach Bryant can.

Willie's favorite souvenirs are footballs autographed by the entire squad. And we're developing a bad case of writer's cramp because of it. On the average, we autograph three to five balls before each meal during the season. The balls are usually sent by alumni, fans, or by charities who sell them at benefit auctions. But with the Liberty Bowl and Coach Bryant's retirement coming up, the number of requests for autographed balls have more than doubled. We signed 14 at lunch alone. And since half of those were brought in by Willie, some of the guys began teasing him about turning a tidy profit by selling the autographed balls.

"How much you selling these for, Mr. Meadows? they would ask.

"Just shut up and sign 'em," he's say. He didn't think our joke was very funny.

But then, he didn't think Dante Bramblett was very funny either when he signed his name in three-inch tall letters on one football. When Willie saw what Dante had done, he turned 20 shades of purple.

"What the hell did you do that for!" Willie demanded to know. "How the hell am I supposed to get 30 more names on that ball when you do that shit!"

"I just wanted everybody to know that I'm still on the roster here," Dante replied with childlike innocence. "Just tell everybody else to write small."

"Write small my ass!" Willie roared as he tried to rub Dante's name off the ball. "Pull this crap again, and your name won't be on the damn roster!"

Dante was still fighting back a laugh as he walked away from the table. "I probably just cost him fifty bucks," he snickered.

December 18

Went Christmas shopping today and couldn't believe all the Alabama and Bear Bryant souvenirs on sale.

I also noticed a new bumper sticker out that reads, "It Took a GIANT To Replace The BEAR." Sounds like the fans are more optimistic than I am.

Attention souvenir hunters! To date, we have signed 432 footballs since the Auburn game. How do I know? Mike McQueen is keeping count.

I noticed Mike writing on the wall next to the equipment cage yesterday, and I asked him what he was doing.

"Just keeping track of how many footballs we have autographed," he said.

I looked up on the wall, and sure enough, there were rows and rows of "stick" markings, all grouped neatly together in bundles of five.

"We signed 26 at dinner last night," Mike said as he made the last mark.

Who says offensive tackles can't count?

December 19

Sunday. Time for some attitude adjustment.

I haven't been terribly fair to Coach Perkins. I've been making all these negative statements and assumptions about the man and I haven't even met him yet. And since we have our first meeting with him tomorrow, I decided it was time I opened my mind and found out more about him.

So I went back and read all about his career here at Alabama—about how he got a serious head injury here and about how he made All-American as a wide receiver on the undefeated 1966 team. I went back and read about his professional career with the Baltimore Colts—how he teamed with Johnny Unitas in two NFL title games and Super Bowls before a knee injury ended his career. And I read all about his coaching experience with Mississippi State, the San Diego Chargers, the New England Patriots, and finally, with the New York Giants. And I must admit, I was impressed by all this.

I really was. I decided I hadn't been fair at all, and I was determined to go into tomorrow's meeting with an open mind, free of prejudice and full of enthusiasm.

But then, someone handed me another newspaper to read, and I became depressed all over again. It was a story in today's *Birmingham News* about the assistant coaches and how most of them would probably be released by Perkins.

Dee Powell, our offensive line coach, was quoted as saying, "We're finished. We're done. It's just a matter of time."

I became so angry that all I could think about were the negative things I had read about Perkins, but had chosen to ignore. I could see us finishing with records as bad as his first two Giant teams. I could see him making and then breaking promises to us just as easily as he did his contract with the Giants. And I could see our offense puttering along at the bottom of the South-eastern Conference the same way the Giants did last year when they finished dead last in the NFL's total offense category.

Dead last. I sure hope I'm dead wrong.

If there's one thing that will really make a player's eyes light up, it's the yearly talk we have with Coach Jim Goostree about transportation expense money for the bowl trip.

Since Goose is not really a coach, but our head trainer, we try to ignore—even avoid him at all costs. But for some unknown reason, he is also charged with informing the team of what we can legally receive in the way of expenses without violating NCAA rules. And so, when Goose talks expense money, he gets more attention than E. F. Hutton.

This year Goose tells us that we have the option of flying on the university's plane to and from Memphis or driving our cars. And that's when you'll see dollar signs flashing in our eyes. Because if you drive your own car, you will be reimbursed the price of the return plane fare plus gas mileage from Tuscaloosa to your hometown. In my case, that will mean I would be getting about $100 for the air fare, plus 16 cents per mile from Tuscaloosa to Mobile. And since it is roughly 200 miles from Tuscaloosa to Mobile, that would be an additional $32 in gas money. Add it up and that is a grand total of about $132. Okay, so it isn't enough to retire on, but it will sure help pay some of my Christmas bills.

Almost everybody I know is driving to Memphis or riding with someone else. And the farther their hometown is from Tuscaloosa, the more money they stand to make. Kurt Schmissrauter, an offensive tackle from Chattanooga, Tennessee, really stands to make a bundle. He will fly into Memphis from Chattanooga in his dad's own Lear jet and fly home afterwards. So everything he makes will be clear profit.

My travel plans are not quite so glamourous. Right now, I'm planning to head home for the holidays after our last practice Tuesday. I'll drive from there to Summit, Mississippi, on

Christmas Day to have dinner with Paul's family. And then we'll head for Memphis, counting the money with each passing mile.

I'll bet you think I know Illinois football inside and out by now. Wrong. Actually, I've hardly seen any films on the ol' Fightin' Illini.

I'm not complaining, mind you. There's nothing I hate more than sitting around for hours watching films of defensive backs taking pot shots at pass receivers. But I do wonder why we aren't seeing more game films on Illinois. I guess the coaches figure there is nothing more we can do to prepare for them. Either that, or they're afraid they will frighten us.

I am very impressed by Illinois' quarterback, Tony "Champaign" Eason. Eason has a very strong arm, and he was a legitimate contender for the Heisman Trophy this year. But I'm not all that worried about him because Jeremiah Castille and Tommy Wilcox can handle just about anything he may throw their way.

Like most good passing teams from the north, Illinois also has a pretty good pass defense. They are deeper in the secondary than any team we've faced this year and have 19 interceptions.

But am I worried, you ask? Some.

December 20

Add one more disaster to my list.

Call it "The Monday Massacre."

The henchman? Ray Perkins, a.k.a. Businessman.

Businessman made his first appearance on campus today. He arrived looking as if he had just stepped from the pages of the *Wall Street Journal.* He was wearing a $330 tailored three-piece suit and shiny black wingtip shoes that must have cost another 80 bucks. His nails were neatly manicured, and not a hair on his well-groomed head was out of place.

I distrusted him immediately.

By the time Businessman had returned to New York, he had unceremoniously stamped out years and years of Alabama tradition, unknowingly divided friends and teammates, and left six good men with more than a century of coaching experience standing in the unemployment line.

OK, so it wasn't as bloody as Bloody Sunday or as heinous as the attack on Pearl Harbor. But, in its own way, what he did today was just as cold, just as unforgivable, because this was just the "business" of coaching.

So what if you did help coach Alabama to four national championships? So what if you did play football here and spent half your adult life coaching here? So what if you have spent the last 20 years working 14 hours a day, seven days a week, 52 weeks a year trying to make Alabama football better?

That's "business." It's hit the road, Jack.

Never mind loyalty. Never mind experience. Never mind that Christmas is just five days away.

Businessman kicked them all out in the cold.

Coach Marks was among the first to be told that he would be out of work in less than a month. Then there was Coach Moore, offensive line coach Dee Powell, defensive line coach Tex Pool, defensive back coach Murray Legg and recruiting coordinator Paul Davis.

And who says the grim reaper carries a scythe and wears a black hooded cloak? He wears a gray three-piece business suit.

Businessman apparently felt there was no need to let us in on his plans. When we met with him early today, he never mentioned that he was going to fire half the staff. He was too busy playing out the role of politician on the campaign trail.

He stood at the front of the meeting room, his hands in his pockets, his head cocked upward with his nose in the air, looking around the room with steely blue eyes that reminded me of a gunfighter. He talked about how much he loved Alabama and Tuscaloosa. He talked about how proud he was to "be back." And he talked about how he wanted us to finish the season by winning the Liberty Bowl.

"Because," he said, "There's no getting around it—you have to win this last one for Coach Bryant."

That last line was the clincher. With that simple declaration of devotion to Coach Bryant, Businessman had charmed half the team into believing he was the only man who could return Alabama football to the Promised Land of unbeaten seasons and national championships.

"This is great!" Paul Carruth said as we left the meeting. "I think he is just what we need."

"Yeah," Doug Vickers said, jumping on the bandwagon, "he seems like a pretty sharp guy all right."

Even Dante Bramblett, who I thought was my most loyal co-conspirator these days, abandoned me.

"He's a pretty cool dude," Dante said, offering the highest compliment he ever gave anyone. "Yep. I like him."

I was almost fooled myself. When he began talking about how much he loved Alabama and Coach Bryant, I considered the possibility that I could be wrong about Perkins. But I wasn't entirely convinced.

So, when Dante pressed further for my opinion of our new leader, I tried to sound as optimistic as possible without sounding overly committed.

"Well," I said, "he's nothing like I had pictured him to be."

But as it turned out, he was *everything* I had thought he would be. I found that out as soon as I walked into the dressing room a couple hours later and found Doug Vickers sitting at his locker in a state of deep depression.

"I guess you have heard about the assistant coaches?" Doug asked.

I hadn't heard, but judging by the tone of Doug's voice, I wasn't sure I wanted to hear either.

"No," I finally said, "what about them?"

"Six of them won't be coming back," he replied. "Coach Perkins broke the news to them right after he met with us."

"Six?!" I said, feeling panicky. "Oh, no. Coach Marks wasn't one of them was he?"

"Yeah," Doug answered, "he was one of them."

"Oh, no!" I said. "Who told you? Are you sure?"

I didn't have to wait for an answer because Coach Marks walked into the room, looking as if he had lost his best friend. I walked over to him slowly.

"Coach Marks," I said, "Is it true you won't be coming back?"

"I'm afraid it is, little buddy," he said.

"Dang!" I said. "Who else?"

He then began listing the names of the dismissed coaches as if he were calling out names of plane crash victims.

"What . . . what are you going to do?" I asked him. "Do you have any plans?"

"No," he replied, "I don't have anything lined up yet. I've got some connections down in Mobile. Maybe I can find something down there."

"You like people down there anyway, don't you?" I asked, trying to smooth things over.

"Yeah," he said. "They are good people down there. But, hey, don't you worry about me, Little Man. I'll be all right."

"I hope so," I said, "but if I can help in any way, just let me know. I want to help if I can."

"Thanks," he said. "I'll remember that."

Coach Marks sounded as upset as I felt. I have been so caught up in my own troubles I had forgotten what the assistant coaches must have been going through. Their problems were much worse than mine. After all, I would at least be given a chance to stay and prove myself to Businessman's new regime—the coaches wouldn't.

Businessman had the nerve to show up at practice after all this. And, of course, it ruined what little concentration we had left.

He took his place in the tower beside Coach Bryant as if he were a king, surveying his newly-acquired inheritance. I wasn't ready to see him standing in Coach Bryant's tower. I know he had every right to be there, to see what kind of team he will be taking over. And I know that Coach Bryant probably thinks Perkins is the right man for the job, or else Perkins wouldn't be here. But, somehow, it still didn't seem right. Maybe it would next week, next month, or maybe even next year—but not now.

I can't help but wonder what Coach Bryant sees in Perkins. They don't seem to have anything in common. Like today, Coach Bryant was dressed as usual in his brown khaki work pants, olive green parka and beige baseball cap. But Perkins was dressed like Clarence Darrow in the same three-piece suit he had worn to the team meeting earlier.

"I wonder," Jimmy Watts said, looking up at them in the tower, "if Perkins ever wears coaching pants. Or does he wear a coat and tie when he's coaching, too?"

"That just must be the New York way," I replied.

"Yeah, maybe," Jimmy said, "but this ain't New York."

More tears today.

We held our last practice at Thomas Field under Coach Bryant and watched the old man climb down from the tower for the last time.

We knew today would be it, the last time we would see him in the tower. I wish we could have given him a better practice to remember us by.

I found myself just standing there, staring up at him in the tower and thinking how nothing will be the same here next season. I thought I was going to cry when Coach Al Miller, our strength coach, walked by and thumped my helmet to awaken me from my trance.

"Better get your mind back down here," he said softly. "He wouldn't want you standing around moping like that."

I just nodded, "Yes, sir," and went back to work.

Coach Perkins didn't waste any time replacing Coach Powell. Today he announced that Tom Goode, the assistant head coach and offensive line coach at Ole Miss, has been hired to take Coach Powell's place.

Coach Powell handled it remarkably well. He was out at practice today, giving it all he's got and still screaming "Dig! Dig! Dig!" at all the linemen.

Mike White said the offensive linemen are really upset about the shoddy treatment of the coaches.

"It looks like Perkins could have waited at least until after the Liberty Bowl before hiring somebody," Mike said.

I agree. It is sort of like the widow remarrying on the day of the funeral. A period of mourning should be allowed, if only for appearance's sake.

I understand Goode is an old friend of Perkins. That's all right. I can see why somebody who has just risen to power would want to let an old friend jump on the bandwagon, too. But I also think you can make a mistake by hiring old friends.

But Ole Miss does have one of the better offensive lines in the Southeastern Conference, so maybe Coach Goode must be doing something right.

I was just reading where Perkins says he plans to hire at least two more assistant coaches with National Football League experience. So it looks more and more like we're turning into Alabama's version of the New York Giants.

And since Perkins says he "doesn't even know what a wishbone is," it looks like the 'bone is going to become a thing of the past.

Actually, I don't mind giving up the wishbone so long as the new offense works. There have been times this year (against Southern Miss for example) when I wish we did have a more wide open offense. Perkins has promised we will have that. He also promises more passing—either out of the veer offense, a drop-back passing scheme, or a complete pro-set offense. But he also says we will still have option plays.

I don't know if I'll ever figure this guy out.

Perkins also says that more and more teams are switching to the passing attack. That's true, and I do like the idea of catching more passes. But I don't think we should change offenses just because it's the fashionable thing to do.

Well, that's about it for now. I've got to get packing and head home to Mobile for a quick Christmas.

December 24
Mobile, Alabama

I'm a prisoner in my own home.

I haven't been able to go anywhere the past two days without people asking me a thousand questions about all that has happened.

"What do you think about Coach Perkins?" they'll ask.

Or, "I guess you're pretty upset about Coach Bryant retiring, huh?"

Or, "Is the team ready for the Liberty Bowl?"

Over and over again, Sometimes, I feel like recording all my answers and when somebody asks a question, I can just whip out my trusty tape recorder and say, "Here, listen to this."

December 25
Memphis, Tennessee

What's that they say about first impressions?

Paul and I strolled into the lobby of the Holiday Inn around 7:30 tonight, covered in Mississippi mud from head to toe.

"My God!" Coach Marks exclaimed when we walked in, tracking mud all over the hotel carpet. "What in the world happened to you two?"

"Well, you see . . ." I said, "It's a long story . . ."

And it really is. But to make a long story short, Paul and I had a small wreck on the trip up. Oh, it wasn't anything serious. We were just zipping right along in the pouring rain when my car began sliding—and sliding—and sliding. Before we knew it, we were planted in the center median, mired in mud up to our bumpers. The car wasn't even damaged and we were not hurt. In fact, the worst thing to come of it was that both of us looked like losers in a mud-wrestling contest.

But when something like this happens, I've learned to milk it for all it's worth. So, I cooked up this great scheme, designed to evoke sympathy from our girl friends, Lindsey Bowers and Elise Lapeyre.

"Wouldn't it be great," I asked Paul, "if we called back home and told them that we'd had a wreck and wouldn't be able to play?

"Well. . .," Paul said, hesitantly. "I don't know—that's a pretty dirty trick."

"I know," I said, "that's what makes it so great! You can call Lindsey and tell her that you've had a wreck and broken your leg. And I'll call Elise and tell her that I've broken my . . . wrist, that's it—I'll tell her I broke my wrist when we wrecked.

"It'll *kill* them. Let's do it."

"Yeah," Paul said, "and when they find out that we're not hurt, they'll *kill* us."

But Paul finally relented and went along with the gag, only on the condition that he could have a badly sprained ankle instead of a broken leg.

"A broken leg," he explained, "is carrying it just a bit too far."

So, as soon as we checked in, we hurried up to our room and began placing the calls.

"Hello, Elise?" I said. "Yeah, we made it all right, but we did have a small wreck on the way up . . . Oh, nothing too bad . . . it was just a small wreck. . .well, yeah, I fractured my wrist but it's OK—honest. I've got a thin cast on it. I'm fine, really. Yeah,

Paul's sort of bruised up, too. . .got a real bad sprained ankle. . .
looks like we'll both miss the game. . ."

She fell for it, and all the while Paul and I were biting our
tongues to keep from laughing. Then, Paul called Lindsey and we
played the charade all over again. Oh, it was a beautiful piece of
acting.

What can I say? The devil made me do it.

On a scale of 1 to 10, our first night out in Memphis
measured a two. It's as cold as I expected, it's still raining, and
there's not one thing to do in Memphis on Christmas night. But
five car loads of us formed a caravan and went roaming around
the empty streets looking for girls or action—or both. We came
up empty-handed. All we found was one hole-in-the-wall beer
joint that was almost deserted. So, we sat there for about three
hours talking about Coach Bryant and how different things are
going to be without him.

December 26

Rain. Rain. Rain. Is that all it does here?

It was still raining this morning so we had to take our first
practice indoors at the the Kennedy Sportsplex on the Memphis
State University campus. But don't be fooled by the fancy name.
The Kennedy Sportsplex is nothing more than a dilapidated old
gymnasium that isn't much good for anything except volleyball
matches.

The Sportsplex has a few cramped dressing rooms and
meeting rooms, but the gym part of it is really pathetic. The
gymnasium is only about 30 yards long, 20 yards wide, and the
ceiling is only about 25-feet high and constructed from low-grade
asphalt.

Once we got inside, the coaches had difficulty deciding what
we could and could not do in such cramped quarters. A full-
scale scrimmage was out of the question. So we stuck to the very
basics—walking through our plays while the defense tried to
intimidate us with blocking dummies. About the only thing you
can evaluate from this kind of practice is who has their mind on
the game and who doesn't. But it does give the coaches an idea of

who knows their assignments.

In that respect, the practice must have been a lot like the one I heard Coach Bryant held in the first-ever Liberty Bowl game back in 1959. The Liberty bowl was held in Philadelphia then, and Alabama was playing Penn State. Still, the new bowl game wasn't getting much attention in the press. So Coach Bryant came up with a great scheme for attracting attention. He asked the Liberty Bowl director to bring 22 folding chairs to practice and then call in the sportswriters. When the writers arrived at practice they found 22 chairs—11 for offense, 11 for defense—sitting face to face with a player in each chair. Coach Bryant would walk around, weaving between the players and calling plays. The players would then point in the direction they were supposed to go on that particular play. The writers loved it. They got their story, and Coach Bryant got his publicity. The next day, the newspapers hailed Coach Bryant as a football genius. Funny thing, though—the reporters never knew that after they left, Coach Bryant had the chairs removed and practice was held as usual.

Things have really changed since then. Now, all Coach Bryant has to do is sneeze and it's automatic headlines. I guess that's the price he has to pay for being successful. But since he announced his retirement, the press has really gotten out of hand.

Today's practice was a zoo. There were so many sportscasters, sportswriters and TV cameramen standing around that we weren't getting anything accomplished.

But one thing you never want to do is make the press mad. We couldn't just ask them to leave us alone, so the coaches found a legitimate excuse. They sent word to the TV reporters that no filming would be allowed of practice, the reason being that they didn't want any offensive formations being aired on television for Illinois to see. So all TV cameras had to be left outside in the hallway. And since a sportscaster and cameraman are virtually useless without their camera, they just left altogether. That cut the sideline crowd in half, and we had more room to work.

But all things considered, I'd say that this was our best Liberty Bowl practice thus far. The short holiday break seems to have been good for us and the coaches. Even Coach Marks and the others who will soon be without jobs appear to be recovering nicely. Some were even laughing.

Coach Bryant is looking really worn out these days. At practice today, he sat on a bench next to the wall in the gym and hardly moved a muscle the whole time. He just sat there staring at the floor, his legs crossed and his shoulders slumping forward. His trusty red bull horn sat on the floor beside him, but he never used it.

He seems bored by this whole thing. His mind seems to be a thousand miles away. I wonder if he is regretting his decision to retire.

Whatever the reason, I hate to see him this way. I'd much rather see him screaming and cursing through that red bull horn—even if it was me that he was screaming and cursing at. That's the "Bear" Bryant the world knows—a mean, tough disciplinarian who can take a sow's ear and make it into a satin pillow. They don't see him the way we do—a man whose hair has turned silvery white, a man whose hands tremble as he lights up another Chesterfield, and a man whose every single step seems slow and calculated. I see these things and I feel sorry I did not know Coach Bryant sooner.

I would give anything—anything at all—to have been one of those who played under him at Texas A&M. I would like to have been one of those 100 A&M players he took out to Junction, Texas, one summer for practices that resembled a Marine boot camp. I don't know whether I would have made it. I might have been like many of those who sneaked out of the camp in the middle of the night. But I would have liked the chance to find out.

Hearing stories about Coach Bryant's years at A&M is a lot like listening to war stories and wishing you had been there. They have a romance about them, an excitement that makes you throw back your head and laugh in appreciation. But most of all, they make you feel warm inside.

Many players who knew Coach Bryant in the late 1950s and early 1960s will say that he put them through hell. But in the end, they'll talk about it as if it were heaven.

Willie Meadows is convinced we're all thieves.

When we got to the Sportsplex this morning, we each found a new set of warmups in our lockers. They were really sharp—crimson red with Alabama written across the chest with white stripes running down both pants legs.

You might find it funny that football players get so excited about a new pair of sweat pants and a sweat shirt. But getting anything like this is rare—very rare. In fact, our usual practice wardrobe consists of any pair of long pants that Willie can dig up and ripped sweat shirts that have 'XXX Large' written across the chest with a black marker.

So getting new sweats was like getting an extra Christmas present. We were all strutting around the dressing room, showing off in them. And that drove Mr. Meadows wild. He couldn't stand the thought of having to keep up with *new* warmup suits.

"Ya'll better not steal them pants," Willie said after we came back from practice.

And just to make sure that we didn't steal them, he stood over us and watched our every move.

"Make sure you put those new sweats back in your locker," he snapped. "I don't want anybody coming to me asking for more because they *lost* theirs."

Don't get the wrong idea about Mr. Meadows. He wasn't behaving like that just because the sweats were new—he acts like that *all* the time. He can get more mileage out of a pair of socks than most people get out of steel belted radials.

A freshman unfamiliar with Mr. Meadows' thrifty ways once approached Willie's equipment cage and requested a different (not *new*, mind you—just different) pair of socks.

"Mr. Meadows," the kid asked, "could I please have a different pair of socks?"

Mr. Meadows took it as a personal insult.

"What for!?" he demanded.

"There's no elastic in these," the kid explained, and held up a pair of sweat socks that looked as if they had been stretched over somebody's head.

"Hell, no," Willie said, "Get outta here. Ain't nothing wrong with them damn socks—they ain't but six years old! Got two good years left in 'em."

The kid knows about Willie Meadows now.

The Liberty Bowl people held a brunch for both teams today, and the Illinois players showed up wearing these dark blue and orange athletic jackets. Mike White and I were standing around talking with this big Illinois lineman and admiring his jacket when another Illinois player walked up.

"Hey, man," he said, tapping me on the shoulder, "aren't you J. J.?"

"Who?" I asked.

"J. J., man," he repeated. "Aren't you J.J.?"

"Ohhh!" I said, realizing that he was referring to my initials, "J. J.—yeah, I'm Joey Jones."

"Yeah, man," he said, "Good to meet ya—I'm M.J. I've seen you on film. You're a pretty good receiver. Fast, too. Looks like we gonna be double-teaming you, man."

"Aw," I said, "you won't need to do that. One person on me will be enough—you probably won't even need one."

As we continued talking I soon found out that M. J. was Mark Jones, a defensive back. And I automatically began telling myself to watch what I said to him. I didn't want to reveal any secret to the enemy. So I changed the subject from football.

"How long you guys been here?" I asked.

"Oh, man, we've been here since before Christmas," he said. "We even had our Christmas here."

"Really?" I said. "Well, it looks like you got a pretty nice jacket for Christmas."

"Yeah," he said, "They gave the whole team one of these jackets and a real nice sweater with Liberty Bowl monogrammed on it. What did you guys get?"

I hated to tell him that we didn't get anything, and I didn't want him to think Alabama was a cheapskate school. So, I nonchalantly mentioned our gas mileage.

"All we got," I said, "was gas mileage from our homes up here and the price of plane fare back."

"Really?" he said, "We get $10 in expenses every day that we're here. What kind of mileage money you getting?"

"Oh, not much," I said. "Everybody on the team is getting at least $425. But I live down in south Alabama and it was a long drive up, so I'll be making around $570 on this trip.

"Five-hundred and seventy dollars!" he said, his eyes bulging.

"Yeah, I know it's not much," I said, shrugging my shoulders, "but that's all they could give us and keep within the rules."

M. J. was in shock. So I decided to relieve some of the

pressure. I stroked the sleeve of his jacket and said, "But that's a great jacket you've got there."

It's Sunday, but the devil in me lives on.

I talked to Elise again on the telephone tonight and carried out my charade of being injured.

"No, honest," I said with my fingers crossed, "it really doesn't hurt much at all."

Paul is wanting us to tell them the truth, but I think I've convinced him to play it out at least one more day. You've got to be tough with these women. . .

December 27

Today's practice was a lot like yesterday's—cramped and crowded. It's been raining here three straight days now, so we had to practice indoors at the Sportsplex again.

Everyone is beginning to feel claustrophobic. We're itching to get back to work. Coach Donahue is about to go stir crazy. He says if the defensive secondary doesn't get a good workout soon, Tony Eason is liable to pick us apart on the passing game. We'll be practicing outside tomorrow come hell or high water. I'll bet it's high water.

Seems like every time we sit down for a meal now we see game films.

"Finished eating?"

"Well, no, I. . .uh. . ."

"Good! Turn your seat around and let's look at some film."

It's enough to give you indigestion.

Headline in today's Memphis paper: "The Game May Be Football—But Bryant's The News."

Good point. Since we've arrived here, the newspapers have been filled with stories of Coach Bryant. It's Bear Bryant did this, or Bear Bryant did that. Even the Illinois fans are beginning to notice. As I was walking through the lobby this afternoon, I passed a couple of Illini fans reading the paper.

"Looks like we've got another Bear Bryant story today," one said to the other.

"I saw that," the other fan replied. "Doesn't this newspaper know there are *two* teams playing in the Liberty Bowl? They hardly ever mention Illinois."

I can't blame Illinois fans for feeling left out. The spotlight has been on Coach Bryant and Alabama ever since he announced his retirement. And while that has created problems for us, Illinois players are also getting caught up in all the hype.

Yesterday as we were getting ready to leave the Kennedy Sportsplex, the Illinois team was getting ready to practice. And when the players saw Coach Bryant walking down the hallway they almost broke their necks trying to get a look at the winningest coach of all time.

The hotel gift shop is filled with Bear Bryant memorabilia and souvenirs. It's a sports collector's paradise—hats, shirts, T-Shirts, belt buckles, car tags, soft drinks, coffee mugs and bumper stickers. Everything for the well-dressed Alabama fan. And, of course, all with the fitting inscription, "Coach Paul 'Bear' Bryant's Last Game, December 29, 1982." Even Coach Goostree's son, Jimmy Tom, is peddling his pencil sketches of Coach Bryant in the hotel lobby.

It is all very exciting to be a part of all this. I really don't mind all the hype about the the game, but in another way, it frightens me. Fans are taking it for granted that we will win this game for The Bear. They haven't stopped to consider that Illinois may want to win this game, too . . .

Sometimes, you just can't tell a woman the truth.

Paul and I broke down and told Lindsey and Elise the truth. "Sur-priise! We're not hurt!"

How did they take the news? Well, let's just say that Paul and I are considering a move to Canada instead of going back to Alabama. Some women just can't take a joke. . .

Just being Coach Paul "Bear" Bryant must be awfully hard. People are always expecting Coach Bryant to be a tower of strength, a man whose grit and determination are inexhaustible. They expect him to be always tough, always demanding. To them, he is a true American hero. And true American heroes, as we all know, never cry.

Coach Bryant cried today.

It happened in a team meeting before practice, our last ever under him. We were sitting in one of the meeting rooms in the Kennedy Sportsplex, joking and laughing, when he entered the room, still wearing the suit he had worn to the luncheon. He closed the door behind him. The room immediately fell silent.

He stood at the front of the room and held a small slip of paper in his hand. He looked down at the paper, cleared his throat, and then looked back at us.

"We need to work on our timing and execution today," he began. "The wishbone ain't worth a damn without it. . .the defense. . .the defense should. . ."

Then, he stopped. He looked down at the paper again, and his eyes became misty. A tear trickled down his cheek. He wiped it away. His hands began to tremble.

I looked at Doug Vickers, who was sitting in the desk beside me, and I could see that Doug was getting choked up, too. Others in the room had stopped looking at Coach Bryant, preferring to gaze at their desktops or shoestrings instead. I felt a lump building inside my own throat and bit my lip to keep from crying.

"Damn it!" Coach Bryant said as he brushed away another tear and looked up. "I wish. . .wish that everyone wasn't making such a big deal out of this game. If I had known it would be like this. . .I would've waited until it was all over to announce my retirement, but it's too late for that now. . .

". . .The press and the fans are expecting you to play this game for me and they are expecting you to win it, too. . .I'm sorry I've put that kind of burden on you. . .it's not fair. . .I. . .I wish I could do something to change the way it is, but I can't.

"You can go out and play this game for me if you want to, and there won't be one damn thing I can do about it. But you have got to be men enough to accept the adversity that you now have. You've got to get back down to business. . .cut out all this whooping 'n hollerin' about winning one for Coach Bryant, and start playing this game for yourselves. . ."

It wasn't the first time I had seen him cry. The first time was Tennessee Week during my freshman year. We were holding our usual Wednesday night meeting with Coach Bryant, and he had opened the meeting in the most general terms. He had talked about what we should expect from Tennessee, what we should look for, and what the game meant to Alabama football.

And then, he started crying. Big tears rolled down his cheeks, but he never flinched. He stood there almost motionlessly, staring straight ahead at us as he continued talking about the game.

A few days later in Knoxville, just minutes before kickoff, Warren Lyles led us onto the field with the charge, "Remember what Coach Bryant said on Wednesday! Let's kick their ass!" And we did. We went out and whipped Tennessee 27-0 on national television. And nobody was prouder of us than Coach Bryant.

That seems like ages ago. And time and translation may have dulled the emotion of that moment. But today's meeting is something I will always treasure. And I will never forget it.

But actually, it was ridiculous for him to apologize for putting so much pressure on us. Maybe we *are* feeling pressure, but it is a self-imposed pressure and that kind of pressure can help you win. So as far as Coach Bryant's apology goes, he can forget it. No apologies needed, Coach. It is all our pleasure.

Wouldn't you know it? There was no rain today. It was almost as if Coach Bryant *willed* the rain away for his last practice. And what a practice it was.

We finally went outside on the Memphis State practice field, and although it was cold and muddy, we enjoyed the heck out of it.

A couple of Coach Bryant's former players, Ricky Watson and Mark Prudhomme, stopped by and stood on the field talking with Coach Bryant for a long time. Several players had the managers to bring their cameras out to the field so they could take pictures of Coach Bryant. The picture-taking continued in the locker room after practice, too. We'd all pile on one another as if we were making a family portait for *Animal House*. Russ

Wood and Scott Homan got some great pictures of Coach Bryant in the locker room, and Coach Bryant seemed to really be enjoying himself at last.

The receivers also presented Coach Marks with his Walkman stereo headphone. I don't know whether he honestly enjoyed the gift itself, but I could tell he appreciated the thought behind it. Still, we didn't want him to remember it as a solemn occasion so we kept things pretty light-hearted.

"You can wear it when you're jogging," we explained. "Tune in on some rock station and maybe it will help you run faster."

He laughed, and so did we.

On the bus after practice we discovered that the Liberty Bowl people had provided each of us with our very own CARE package. It was a box full of cheap freebies—toothpaste, deodorant, a solar calculator, and—get this—a pair of panty hose. We immediately decided that we must uphold the Joe Namath tradition and wear the panty hose during the game tomorrow night.

Walking through the hotel lobby late this afternoon I heard this conversation between two Illinois fans:

"I wish we were playing anybody except Alabama tomorrow night," said one.

"Oh? Why is that?" the other fan asked.

"Because I kind of like Bear Bryant," the first fan replied, "and I sure would like to see him go out a winner."

Mike Adcock was attacked by Green Monsters last night, and it took half the day for him to recover. Green Monsters are really nasty.

And what are Green Monsters, you ask?

Green Monsters are a drink that Mike discovered last night at an Irish club called *Silky Sullivan's*. The Green Monster is served in something that resembles a five-gallon paint bucket. Quite naturally, it is green. It contains rum, creme de menthe and a variety of other poisonous liquors. It also costs somewhere around $15 a pop, tip included. And needless to say, the Green Monster has a bite to it.

Due to the expense involved, we figured Mike would be safe from the Green Monster. But we were wrong—once the Green Monster gets you, it doesn't let go. It didn't help matters any when an inebriated Alabama fan showed up at the club and began buying rounds for everyone.

I can't say for certain how the evening ended up, but I do remember having nightmares about green monsters buying drinks for a roomful of people wearing houndstooth hats and singing "Yea, Alabama!" with an Irish accent.

Time to get serious. We had a team meeting tonight—team as in players only, as in no coaches allowed.

Several players felt we should talk about this game and straighten out our priorities. Todd Roper, Mike Pitts and Jeremiah Castille all took turns getting a few words in, but Jeremiah said it best.

"Look," Jeremiah said, "I know how everybody here feels about winning this game for Coach Bryant. That's the way it should be— he *should* win his last game. That's only right.

"But we can't lose sight of what we're supposed to be doing out there tomorrow night. Sometimes, you can get so wrapped up in playing for someone else that you forget that you should also be playing for yourself. If you're out there thinking about Coach Bryant and not thinking about the game, you're going to make mistakes. You won't be playing like you're capable of playing. But if you're out there playing for yourself, doing your job the way it's supposed to be done, the game will take care of itself. So, win it for Coach Bryant, but play it for yourself."

Amen, Jeremiah, amen.

Elise is still angry at me for "lying" (that's the word she used) about being hurt. I tried to explain to her that it wasn't a "lie," it was just a joke. She still couldn't understand how I could do such a thing. I've never even met her parents, but she says they think that I'm the biggest liar in the whole state of Alabama. Then I explained that I'm not a liar—Paul is. Ouch! Just kidding, Paul.

On most nights before a big game, I'll spend a few minutes alone in the dark thinking about nothing but the game. I'll try to picture myself out on the field, running a pass route or catching the ball. I try to create an image in my mind of what it will be like once we actually get on the field, and I'll go back over any new plays we might have put in for the game. This has almost become a ritual with me, and I believe it really helps my concentration in the game.

But tonight my ritual just isn't working. I can't seem to fool myself into believing that this is just another football game. My mind knows better. Every time I close my eyes and try to see the football falling gently into my hands, all I can see is Coach Bryant's weathered face.

December 29

Quick note before we leave for the stadium: Coach Bryant says he's a senior this time—it's his last game, too.

He looked awfully sad when he said it, but at least he wasn't crying.

Well, that's about all I have time for—got to go win one more for The Bear.

December 30

Paul and I crossed the Mississippi state line a half hour ago. We've had two hours' sleep and too much beer. Our eyes look like road maps of New York City, and our heads are buzzing like two bees in a jug. The price of victory does not come cheap.

But are we happy? Darn right!

We won! We Won! We won! Yeee-Haawww!

Oh, it was bee-yoo-tiful! The crowds, the noise, the offense, the defense—everything was terrific. You couldn't have asked for a better ending to Coach Bryant's career. Yes, we were fan-tastic! But why *should* I be modest about it? We were fabulous, stupendous, and amazing all rolled into one. Get the idea?

I'm not saying it was easy—far from it. The panty hose we received in our Libery Bowl CARE packages saved out butts from frostbite. And the defense saved our behinds from losing the game. The score was 21 to 15, not an overpowering margin, but still the kind of score that Coach Bryant prefers. He doesn't like those boring, lopsided 40-to-nothing scores any more than I do, and he wants us to earn everything we get. And we certainly earned this one.

It seems as if we spent most of our drives punting the ball away, while Illinois spent most of its time watching Jeremiah Castille intercept Eason's passes. It became one of the hardest-hitting football games I've ever played. The defense knocked Eason out of the game on three different occasions. Russ Wood and Tom McCrary hit him so hard one time that his eyes bulged out and then crossed.

Each time Eason went out, a back-up quarterback named Kris Jenner took his place. Jenner ran only three plays all night—all were passes, and all were intercepted. Robbie Jones picked off Jenner's third pass to end Illinois' last threat. All that was left was to run out the clock. That's when I knew we had done what we had come here for. We had won for Coach Bryant.

Some fans counted down the seconds; others chanted "We Love Bear! We Love Bear!" The band struck up the fight song, and after they finished it, they began playing "Auld Lang Syne."

I felt a tear roll down my cheek as Jackie Cline, Larry Brown and Chuck McCall hoisted Coach Bryant onto their shoulders and carried him to the middle of the field to shake hands with Coach White. I tried to move closer, but by then, the field was covered with fans. And more fans were climbing over the fences.

We moved to the end zone where the Liberty Bowl officials presented Jeremiah a trophy for most valuable player and handed Coach Bryant the bowl trophy. I looked around and saw Steve Mott and Jackie Cline crying. But both were smiling. I saw Coach Moore and Coach Campbell run off the field. They, too, were crying.

The locker room was a madhouse. Russ Woods climbed on

top of a bench, wearing nothing but his jock strap. He waved a towel around and around over his head and yelled, "Awww riiight! We did it! We did it!" Or something like that. Other players were taking pictures for their scrapbooks, while the rest hammed it up in front of the cameras by piling on top of one another like a pyramid. Some players were dancing around in the aisles naked.

Coach Bryant began walking through the room, stopping at every locker and hugging every player. When I saw him working his way toward me, I began trying to prepare some sort of short speech in my head—to tell him how much I enjoyed playing for him. The next thing I knew he was hugging my neck and patting me on the back.

"Nice game, Little Man," he said.

"Thanks, Coach, I said.

Before I could say anything else, he had moved on down the line to Jesse Bendross. "Oh, well," I thought, "I can tell him later."

The dressing room was then opened to the press, and the room became so crowded you could hardly breathe. Steam from the showers filled the room like a heavy fog. The television reporters and their cameramen tried interviewing several players. but the steam kept fogging over their camera lens. There would be no locker room interviews on this night. But it didn't matter—we had won.

Afterwards, we partied all night long. We deserved it. Paul and I didn't make it back to the hotel until 4:30 this morning, and we were up and packing shortly before 7 a.m.

So, here we are—cruising down the Mississippi back roads headed home again. The sun is shining for the first time in almost a week. Every now and then a car or van with Alabama license plates will pass and toot its horn at us. One that just passed had a bumper sticker that read, "The Tide Just Keeps Perkin' Along."

Keep it between the ditches, Paul. . .

PART V

Does Heaven Need A Coach?

January 2, 1983
Mobile, Alabama

Ahhhh. There really is no place like home, especially on a Sunday afternoon. And especially on a Sunday afternoon after the season is over.

When you've put away your shoulder pads and helmets at the end of a season, you gain this wonderful feeling of freedom. You have done your job—maybe not as well as you had hoped, but at least it is over and done with. You are ready for a long-needed rest.

Back at Bryant Hall in Tuscaloosa, Sundays don't mean much at all. You wake up feeling as if you've been run over by a bread truck. Every bone and muscle in your body is aching. There is always a bruise somewhere that wasn't there the day before. But you have to get out of bed just the same because there are team meetings to attend. There are game films to be watched. There are weights to be lifted. There are injuries to be treated. There is always something. . .

It's not like that at home. Sunday mornings at home mean lying in bed after the alarm clock has sounded—if you bothered to set the alarm in the first place. Sunday mornings mean you can do whatever you want—visit an old school chum, take a trip to Gulf Shores and lie around on the beach, or just lie around in bed and snooze your life away. Today, I chose the latter of the three evils.

One reason I'm so worthless today is that yesterday was New Year's Day. And everyone knows there's nothing much to do on

New Year's Day except sit around, drink beer and watch all the bowl games on television. It's an American tradition. I did my celebrating at a friend's house where we just sat around, guzzled beer, and watched Penn State beat Georgia and Herschel Walker 27-23 in the Sugar Bowl.

In one way, watching the Sugar Bowl made me mad because I felt like we should be playing there, not Georgia. But in another way, watching "them 'Dawgs" lose was the next best thing to being there.

The way I see it, Georgia's defeat puts us in a good position to claim the national championship. Confused? Don't be.

It's a case of simple arithmetic: (1) Georgia was ranked No. 1 and unbeaten, but (2) Penn State beat Georgia, and now (3) we are the only team in the nation to beat Penn State.

Presto! We're the national champs! Don't you just *love* the polls?

I slept until almost noon. Then I heard my mother banging pots and pans in the kitchen, and I smelled her seafood gumbo cooking. Nobody—and I mean *nobody*— can prepare seafood gumbo they way Mom can. And if I can't hook on with the NFL or USFL after this season, I may just decide to go into business marketing Mom's gumbo.

Since Dad died in 1974 and left Mom with a skinny 12-year-old to feed, she has been father, mother and big brother to me. She spent several years working two jobs just trying to keep food on the table, clothes on my back, and bill collectors away from the door.

Most of the time it has been Mom and me against the world. But there were other times when she demanded that I stand alone, like the time when I was an undersized 13-year-old on a Babe Ruth baseball team. One of the bigger kids kept pushing me around in practice. I came running home to mother, crying about the big kid who was picking on me. That's when Mom put her foot down.

"Don't you ever run away from a fight!" she scolded me. "You stand up for your rights."

"But, Mom," I pleaded, "he's a lot bigger than me."

"That doesn't matter," she replied. "As small as you are, if you run from a fight now, you'll be running the rest of your life."

As usual, she was right.

The next day I had an opportunity to test Mom's advice. The big kid refused to leave the batting cage and let me take batting practice. When I stepped in front of him, he punched me in the back with his bat.

One thing led to another. Insult was traded with insult. Shove was met with shove. Within seconds, I had the big kid pinned to the ground with my knees and was working furiously on his face with both fists. I could feel his teeth cutting into my knuckles with each blow, but I was so afraid of what he may do if I let him up that I just kept punching harder and harder. It wasn't until the team gathered around to watch the show that my coach saw us fighting. He rushed over and pulled me off the big kid. My knuckles were bleeding, but so was his mouth. I wasn't afraid any more.

I never had any more trouble with that big kid. I rushed home after practice and gave my Mom a blow-by-blow account of my fight. She hugged me, tended my bleeding knuckles, and afterwards we celebrated over a bowl of seafood gumbo.

The 10 o'clock newscast showed scenes of New York Giants players carrying Ray Perkins off the field on their shoulders. The Giants beat the Eagles 26-24, but lost out on a bid for the NFL play-offs.

Let's see now. . .the Giants finished the strike-shortened season with a 4-5 record, miss the NFL playoffs, and they still carry Perkins off the field? And weren't most of those players smiling? Hmmm. . .sounds like they're awfully glad to get rid of him.

In other news from New York, Perkins says he doesn't want to take the athletic director's job when Coach Bryant surrenders that title too.

"I don't think any one man can be athletic director and head coach and do a good job," Perkins said.

Gee, I thought Coach Bryant handled both jobs rather well, didn't you?

January 3

Chalk one up for the working man.

Bruce Arians, our running back coach and one of the few asked to stay on, has apparently told Perkins what to do with the job.

Arians was named head coach at Temple University yesterday, succeeding Wayne Hardin who resigned at the end of this season.

I didn't even know Coach Arians was looking for another job. But I'm happy for him. He has always been a favorite with the players, mainly because of his style.

Paul Carruth won't be too happy about this though. He was feeling rather safe, knowing that Coach Arians would be back next season. But now, it looks like Paul is going to have to start all over again just like me.

January 5

The buddy system is alive and well in Tuscaloosa.

Just heard on the radio that Perkins has hired two more friends as assistant coaches for the defense. They are Rockey Felker and Dave Rader.

Felker was a quarterback when Perkins was an assistant at Mississippi State, and Rader was a back-up quarterback with the New York Giants. More recently, however, Felker has spent the last two years at that great football power known as Memphis State where he coached quarterbacks and receivers. Meanwhile, Rader has been polishing his football knowledge at some oil company in Tulsa, Oklahoma.

The radio report failed to mention what positions Rader and Felker would be coaching. But I imagine one of them will be my next receivers' coach. I guess I'll discover which one soon enough.

January 10
Bryant Hall

Who is afraid of the big bad wolf?

Nobody.

At least Mike McQueen isn't afraid. And I could hug his neck for it.

Our first day back at the salt mines was marked by a very interesting meeting with our new slave drivers—Ray "Businessman" Perkins and his two sidekicks, Rockey Felker and Dave Rader.

Once the initial introductions and preliminaries were out of the way, we got down to the serious issues that had been gnawing away at many of us. And it was up to Mike McQueen, an offensive tackle from Enterprise and our duly appointed team spokesman, to bring up the tough questions.

"What about dormintory rules?" Mike asked, raising his hand. "Will these be changing or staying the same?"

Perkins looked puzzled. His eyebrows arched in surprise and then met in a frown. Perkins looked directly at Mike, staring into his eyes. This was the game—a showdown, a contest of will power to see who would be the first to turn his eyes away. Mike held his ground, and Perkins finally answered.

"Most will be staying the same," Perkins finally replied. "Of course, there may be just a few changes. . .I don't know yet. I'll get the rules typed up and passed out as soon as I can."

There—that wasn't so bad. And Perkins was actually quite civil about it.

Mike pressed further.

"And what about curfew?" Mike asked, this time more boldly. "What will it be?"

Surprisingly, Perkins didn't even hesitate this time.

"I don't know yet," he said, throwing his shoulders back in a shrug. "I haven't decided, but I think it will be something we can all live with."

The answers were not exactly what we had been hoping for. But by just asking the questions, Mike had taken that important first step in establishing the player-coach relationship. It's a feeling out process—sizing up one another, searching for the vulnerable areas, and generally, seeing just how much you can get by with without setting off the alarm that may transform this cool, callous businessman into a swearing, screaming football coach.

We didn't have that problem with Coach Bryant. With him, we always know where we stand—and it's on his home turf. Nobody would have dared ask Coach Bryant the questions Mike had just asked, not unless they had lost all sanity. Team meetings

with Coach Bryant were really quite simple in the ground rules—
he talked, you listened.

Not that anybody minded. With Coach Bryant, you *wanted*
to listen. You *wanted* to hear what he had to say, and you hung
onto every mumbled syllable no matter how trivial or unimportant it may seem. Poetry readings were commonplace.

One of my favorite team meetings with Coach Bryant went
something like this: He shuffled into the room, wearing his baggy
trousers and tennis shoes, and carrying a sheet of notebook
paper.

"I've got a little ditty for you here," he said, beginning the
way he always did when he had a poem to read. "It's a poem
written by Walter Wintle and it's called, 'It's All in a State of
Mind':

> *'If you think you are beaten, you are;*
> *If you think you dare not, you won't;*
> *If you like to win, but don't think you can,*
> *It's almost a cinch you won't.*
>
> *'If you think you'll lose, you're lost;*
> *For out in the world you'll find*
> *Success begins with a fellow's will;*
> *It's all in a state of mind.*
>
> *'For many a game is lost*
> *Ere even a play is run.*
> *And many a coward fails*
> *Ere even his work is begun.*
>
> *'Think big and your deeds will grow,*
> *Think small and you'll fall behind;*
> *Think that you can and you will;*
> *It's all in a state of mind.*
>
> *'If you think you are out-classed, you are;*
> *You've got to think high to rise;*
> *You've got to be sure of yourself before*
> *You can ever win a prize.*

After he finished (and he didn't look it the paper very often because he apparently knew it by heart), Coach Bryant folded the paper and put it into his shirt pocket.

"I'll be danged if that ain't true," he said, shaking his head in childlike wonder.

This particular scene was acted out literally hundreds of times during the past three years. And I understand that the same thing was taking place here long before I ever arrived.

But always, always, you could count on Coach Bryant to begin and end his recitations the same way—"Got a little ditty for you here. . ." and "I'll be danged if that ain't true. . ."

After each of these readings I would always find myself sitting there thinking about what he had said, and wondering if he had intended that poem to be just for me. And I would think about that poem for days afterward, which is what Coach Bryant wanted us to do in the first place.

Team meetings with Coach Bryant were not without humor, though. Earl Collins (remember Earl?) loved the meetings so much that he always tried to sit on the front row. Unfortunately for Earl, the tiny desks we have to sit in are so uncomfortable that Earl would lean back and stretch his long legs out, dangling them in the aisle. Coach Bryant noticed this as he entered the room. He stopped, looked down at Earl's feet hanging out from the tiny desk, and frowned.

"Damn, Earl! he said, "If your feet get any bigger we're gonna have to carry you down to the crossroads just so you can turn around."

And there were times when you dared not laugh at all, regardless of how funny things may seem. One such time occurred last year, just two days before the 315th game with Auburn.

We were sitting around in the meeting room, laughing and talking as we waited for Coach Bryant to arrive. All of us, that is, except Bob Cayavec and Gary Bramblett. Bob and Gary had been caught raising hell at a local nightclub the night before, and both were hoping to avoid Coach Bryant for another day or so until he had a chance to cool down. They had carefully chosen seats in the back of the room, hoping to hide from Coach Bryant's line of fire.

Suddenly, the double doors leading into the room flew open, and Coach Bryant burst into the room like he was leading a commando raid. His face was flushed with anger, his eyes were pressed into slits. But he had come into the room so quickly that his feet almost slipped from under him. He began flailing his arms as he tried to keep his balance . And with one leg kicked into the air, he looked more like one of the Rockettes than an angry football coach. We bit our lips to keep from laughing. But Bob and Gary sunk even lower in their seats.

It was too late. Coach Bryant had regained his balance, but not his temper. And his eyes zeroed in on Bob and Gary.

"Bob Cayavec and Gary Bramblett!" Coach Bryant thundered. "Go to my office right now!"

Ahhh, those were the days. . .

Today's meeting with Perkins wasn't near as much fun. In fact, it was no fun at all. After Mike got the ball rolling, others began asking questions—about the offense, about spring practice, etc., etc. And Perkins seemed to take each question as a personal affront. He would lock those gunfighter's eyes on the questioner, and if it was a question he did not like, he would shoot back with, "What?" just to make you ask the question again. Other questions he answered with a short, "Nope." Either he is trying to intimidate us, or he is deaf and has very limited vocabulary. Or both.

Unfortunately, many of our questions remain unanswered. The meeting was short, lasting about about 20 minutes. And even that length of time seemed to be an imposition on Perkins' valuable time.

"I've got to get going," he said, looking at his watch. "I'm running late. I'll be on the road recruiting for the next few days, but when I get back, we'll get started on the X's and O's."

X's and O's?

The highlight of this meeting, if you can call it that, was the introduction of Felker and Rader as the newest additions to the coaching staff.

Perkins says Rader will be coaching the receivers, another prospect that doesn't excite me.

Rader is a tall, lanky guy whose body is built out of right angles. He's 25 going on 35, has the arms and legs of a spider monkey, and a pointed nose that glows like Big Bird's beak. Throw in an army haircut with Buster Brown bangs hanging down and ears that stick out like car doors, and you have it—a younger version of Coach Ken Donahue.

I took one look at him and leaned over to Paul Carruth and whispered, "Oh, no! We've done got ourselves an offensive coach Ken Donahue!"

"You're right," Paul giggled. "He'll probably have you out there doing grass drills after practice!"

Felker, on the other hand, has the country charm of Huck Finn. He would seem more at home in a pair of overalls and lying under a haystack than he would in bright red warmup pants and tennis shoes.

But Felker is Paul's childhood hero. Paul says he grew up watching Felker quarterback Mississippi State teams, and he believes Felker will be a great addition to the staff. Who am I to tear down boyhood idols?

After the meeting ended, Paul went up to introduce himself to Felker and shake hands. I slipped quietly out the door.

One final observation: This was our first real meeting without Coach Bryant as head coach. I wonder if he missed the meeting as much as we missed him?

January 11

Heard that Coach Marks was on campus today so I went over to the Athletic Department to see him. But when I got to his office, he wasn't there. The top of his desk had been cleaned off. The walls, once covered with pictures of former players and All-Americans, were bare. The contents of his desk had been emptied into a cardboard box sitting on the floor.

I lingered in the doorway, looking at what had once been Coach Marks' office. Ten long, hard years of work had ended and now filled a single cardboard box. I thought about all the changes that have been taking place, and I felt angry.

As I turned away from the office door, my eyes met Coach Bryant's. He had been standing in the hallway watching me. I felt myself blushing. Can he read minds, *too?*

"Oh, hello, Coach," I said and walked toward him.

"How are you doing, Little Man?" he said.

He put his arm around my shoulders and we walked down the hallway.

"I don't suppose Coach Marks is still here, is he?" I asked. "I was wanting to see him before he leaves."

"No," he said, "he isn't gone yet. I think he's down in the parking lot putting some things in his car."

Then he got quiet. His eyes that used to scare me, looked so sad. I could tell something was bothering him.

"Are you doing okay, Coach?" I asked.

"Oh, I'm doing fine," he said. "Don't you worry about me. I wish it would warm up, though. I'd like to get some fishing in. You do much fishing?"

"Not a lot," I said, "But I like to go every once in a while."

"Well, Paul Junior has a pond down on his farm stocked with catfish as big as your arm," he said and chuckled. "When it warms up, we ought to go out there and catch us some."

"Yes, sir, I'd like that."

And I really would. But I also know that it will probably never happen. He will probably forget, and I'll never get up the courage to ask him again.

January 12

I got to thinking about Coach Bryant and the conversation we had yesterday. And I realized that of all the pictures I've had him autograph, I've never gotten one for myself.

I have an 8-by-10 glossy of him leaning against the goal post in his houndstooth hat, and I'd like to get it personally autographed. Maybe something like, "To Little Big Man — My Greatest Player Ever. Best Wishes, Coach Bryant." Just joking of course.

So between classes today, I stopped by the Athletic Department again. I carried the picture of Coach Bryant hidden inside my notebook. As I approached Coach Bryant's office, I could see the door was open. Inside, I could see him sitting at his desk, shuffling through a stack of papers about two feet high. His reading glasses were resting on the end of his nose. A Chesterfield was burning in the ashtray.

I stood several feet from the door, trying to summon up enough nerve to knock. He must have sensed me standing there because as I began to turn away, he looked up and peered over the top of his reading glasses at me.

"You need to see me, Little Man?" he asked.

I didn't want to bother him now. He was busy enough without some player hounding him for an autograph.

"Uh. . .no, Coach," I said, clutching my notebook and backing away from the door. "Er, uh. . .I. . .I was just going to see if Coach Marks was around. Sorry to have disturbed you."

I walked on down the hall toward Coach Marks' office, hoping that by some chance I would see him. I was too late. The office was empty.

January 17

Good news does travel fast.

Ray Perkins made his best move in 20 years today when he hired George Henshaw away from Florida State to be our new offensive coordinator.

I met Coach Henshaw back when I attended Bobby Bowden's summer football camp at Florida State several years ago, and I immediately took a liking to him. I also believe that Henshaw is the main reason FSU has done so well these past couple years. This past season alone, FSU averaged 35.2 points per game (second in the nation) and 465.7 yards total offense per game (third in the nation).

I had heard that Perkins had hired him and I had read an announcement about Coach Henshaw on the bulletin board in Bryant Hall, but I didn't get to see him again until today at lunch. I was sitting there with Paul, wolfing down the last of my salad when I saw this bright movement in the corner of the cafeteria. I looked over and saw this man wearing red-green-and-yellow plaid knit slacks, yellow turtleneck shirt and green leisure coat. There is only one man I know who dresses that way—George Henshaw.

I thought about walking over to re-introduce myself to him,

but I didn't think he would remember me. As it turned out, he not only remembered me but came over to my table to say hello.

"How's it going, Joey?" he asked, offering his hand for a handshake. I obliged.

"Pretty good, Coach," I said, "Congratulations and welcome aboard."

"Thanks," he said and smiled. "Things working out pretty well for you here I see. We'd sure liked to have gotten you down at Florida State."

"Well," I said, blushing. "You know how it is—just felt like I needed to stay in the state."

"Well, we would've sure liked to have gotten you. You know how Coach Bowden believes in throwing those long bombs. You could have caught yourself a ton of 'em down there."

"Yeah, I guess I could have at that," I said. "But I've been happy here just catching those 10-yard out passes."

"Well, we might just be opening it up a little more for you now," he said and laughed.

"Oh, yeah? What kind of offense are we going to be running anyway?" I asked.

"It's not set, yet," he said. "I imagine it will be a cross of what we ran at Florida State and what Coach Perkins ran with the Giants. I'm not sure. Coach Perkins is still out recruiting, but I hope to be getting with him soon because I need to know something, man."

After a while, we shook hands again, offered one another good luck, and he left. I sat at the table beaming from ear to ear.

"Wow!" Paul said. "Did you see that outfit he was wearing?"

"Yeah," I said laughing. "Looked sort of like a vacuum cleaner salesman, didn't he?

"But he's a great offensive coach. I really liked him down at the Florida State camp. Man, I can't believe he remembered me after all this time! He even remembered my name!"

"Well," Paul said, "since you didn't go to Florida State, it looks like they'll be bringing Florida State to you."

This season may not be so bad after all.

January 20

Ray Perkins must not be half the businessman I thought he

was—not unless you call taking a $200,000 pay cut "good business."

I just read a report that the Associated Press picked up from the *Selma Times-Journal* on salaries of Southeastern Conference coaches and presidents, and Perkins is at the top of the list. According to the paper, Perkins is making $100,000 a year, the same amount Coach Bryant supposedly makes and $25,000 a year more than Dr. Joab Thomas, the university president, earns.

It surprises me that the university would pay Perkins this much, considering that he is still virtually unproven as a college coach. But at the same time, it surprises me that Perkins would take the job for that amount. I've read somewhere that Perkins was making $300,000 a year with the Giants, and if that's the case then he must not be as money hungry as I had him figured to be. It says a lot that he would give up $200,000 a year just to come back and coach at Alabama.

Another surprise in this report is that Pat Dye is only making $54,180 a year as Auburn's coach. That's quite a gap between Alabama and Auburn there. It also says that Auburn's president, Hanly Funderburk, makes $78,461 a year—I wonder what the $1 is for?

Vince Dooley at Georgia comes closer to Perkins' salary than anybody in the SEC at $85,000 a year. It's no wonder he turned Auburn down. The lowest paid coach in the SEC is Jerry Claiborne at Kentucky, which doesn't surprise me since all they care about up there is basketball.

January 22

Where have you gone, Ray Perkins?

Nobody around here seems to know, and we're not too happy about it either. A lot of players are complaining because Perkins is never here. We want to know something about this new offense and soon. Time is running out. Spring practice is less than two months away and we still don't know a darn thing about what we're going to be doing. We haven't seen Perkins in two weeks.

Joe Carter, a running back from Starkville who is good friends with Paul, stopped by our room today and was airing his gripes about it. The conversation went something like this:

Joe: "Have you seen Coach Perkins around lately?"

Paul: "No. I guess he's still out recruiting."

Joe: "Recruiting is fine, but it looks like he could leave some of it up to the assistants. I wonder when we're going to get our new offense in. Damn, this is ridiculous. If we've got to learn a whole new offense, this is the time to do it. We've got to start learning it sometime."

Paul: "That's right. I'm tired of waiting."

January 25

Close call tonight.

Paul and I were in our room listening to the radio when the announcer broke in with a report that Coach Bryant was admitted to Druid City Hospital a couple hours ago complaining of chest pains. Paul and I froze.

"Oh, God," I thought. "Don't let it be true."

Then they had an interview with Coach Bryant's doctor, who said that "there is absolutely nothing to be alarmed about." But we didn't breathe again until after the interview was over.

Paul says we should send him some flowers, and I agree. And if he is still in the hospital tomorrow night, we're going to see him.

February 15

George Daniel Jones hated to lose. With him, winning was the only way to live. That's how I remember my father.

Even when he was in his early 50s and smoking far too many cigars for a man who had already had two heart attacks, he would challenge me to race him to the convenience store a half block from my house.

"Bet I can beat you to the store," he'd yell, and take off running.

But before I could say, "No, you can't," he would be halfway there. Okay, so he didn't always play it fair and square, but he always won. Always.

The only thing I ever beat my Dad in was a game of table tennis. And that happened only once because he would never play me again.

Sore loser? Sure.

He came to watch me play in a Pee Wee football game at Maitre Park one afternoon, and I was determined to impress him. I was a 50-pound running back, but when my team neared the goal line, I carried the ball. I gave it all I had. I took off running around right end where I met a 75-pound defensive tackle head on. We hit so hard that both our K-Mart brand helmets cracked and split wide open. The big tackle fell backwards and I fell forward across the goal line with my ears ringing. After the game, Dad put his arms around my shoulders and we walked back to the car.

"That was some play you made out there," he said. "Most people would've run away from that big ol' boy, but you didn't. You don't back down from anything, do you?"

When Dad decided I was old enough to graduate from a B.B. gun to a pellet rifle, I was so thrilled that I carried my new rifle everywhere I went. And I mean everywhere. That, of course, came in real handy one day when we went on a family outing across Mobile Bay Bridge to Daphne. We were sitting at a drive-in restaurant having lunch when I saw a flock of black birds in a pasture across the street. I immediately began begging Dad to let me go test my marksmanship on the birds. It was obvious he didn't want me to go, but he reluctantly escorted me through the traffic just the same.

By the time we had reached the fence, however, the birds had flown away. Dad was relieved, but I was still an 8-year-old boy with a loaded pellet rifle and an itchy trigger finger. So, as Dad turned back toward the street and waited for the traffic to clear, I searched for a new target. That's when I saw an old mule grazing nearby.

"Ah ha!" I thought to myself, "A victim!"

I quickly glanced at Dad again, just to make certain he wasn't watching me. Then, I aimed squarely at the mule's hindquarters. (Where else would you think an 8-year-old boy would aim?) Smiling, I squeezed the trigger.

Bingo! A direct hit!

The mule went crazy. Kicking high in the air twice, the mule began running around that pasture. It leaped over the fence and into the highway where a car had to swerve off the road and into a ditch trying to avoid the mule.

I looked up at Dad who was standing there watching with his mouth hanging open.

"I wonder what got into that mule?" he said to me.

"I dunno, Dad," I said innocently, "He must've gone crazy or something."

Dad would have never known what had caused all the ruckus and near wreck if it had not been for Mom, who had seen the whole thing from our car across the street. After she told Dad what I had done, it was all over for me and my big game hunting. Weeks later, we laughed about it.

Then came the night of September 6, 1973. Mom and Dad were sitting on the living room sofa and I was lying on the floor with my head in my hands watching TV. Suddenly, Dad began gasping for air and clutching at his chest. His eyes rolled back as he lurched forward and fell to the floor beside me. His dentures had fallen halfway out of his mouth. I didn't know what was happening to Dad, but it scared me. I ran out of the room screaming and then stood crying and watching Dad. My mother was crying as she kneeled over him, trying frantically to revive him.

She called the ambulance, but it seemed to take forever. Seconds turned into minutes, minutes into an hour. We could hear the ambulance's sirens coming in the distance, and finally we could see the flashing red lights. But the ambulance *didn't* stop. It passed the house and continued speeding on down the street. It had *missed* our house. Before the ambulance driver realized his mistake and returned, it was too late. Daddy had died.

I didn't go to the funeral. Mom said it would have been too hard on a 10-year-old. My sister took me to lunch to try to take my mind off the funeral. It didn't help.

We buried Dad about 40 miles from our home. The cemetery is on the same road I travel whenever I go to Gulf Shores for the weekend. Usually, I stop by to visit him. I sometimes think I don't visit often enough.

I don't know why I'm telling you this. I guess it's because Dad has been on my mind a lot lately. So has death.

I don't handle death very well. I don't know of anybody who does. But death isn't any easier for me now than it was when I was 10. I hope I never have to get used to it.

That's why I've neglected my notes and tape recorder since Coach Bryant died. Writing a book has been the last thing on my mind. It's been a very hard three weeks for me and everybody else in Bryant Hall.

One thing about death, though, is that it makes you realize just how precious life really is. When someone dies, the first reaction is to recall the last time you saw the person alive. You take that day and hold onto it tightly for fear that you may lose the memory too. You try to remember the expression on their face, something they said or did. Or you remember some silly little insignificant detail and try to draw some grand parallel between it and the day they died.

When I last saw Coach Bryant he was sitting at his desk working. That was the day I went up to get his autograph but chickened out. I'm sorry I did now. Paul and I never got to visit him in the hospital because he died the following afternoon.

It was around 2 o'clock in the afternoon when I first heard about it. Mike Adcock and I were driving out to The Corner to play video games when we heard the bulletin on the car radio. We rode along for two or three blocks without speaking before I finally asked Mike if he thought it was true.

"I don't know," he said. "They said he was all right last night. . . .damn!"

Mike pulled a u-turn in the street and we sped back to Bryant Hall. By the time we arrived, both of us were crying. They never made an official announcement to the team that Coach Bryant had died. There was no need for it.

The dorm that day seemed almost spooky. Everybody talked in whispers or they didn't talk at all. Upstairs, it was even worse. The only sound you heard was the crackle of static on radios as players listened to reports of Coach Bryant's death. Many of us tried to call home but found the phone lines tied up.

Paul and I sat in our room listening to a special report on WUAL-FM. According to their reports, Coach Bryant's heart stopped beating around 12:40 p.m. The doctors then put a needle-like pacemaker through his chest and were able to restore a weak heartbeat. It just wasn't enough. The heart attack he had had two years earlier had weakened the heart muscle and arterial sclerosis had set it. He never had a chance. At 1:30 he died. Mary

Harmon and Coach Campbell were with him when he died of "massive coronary occlusion."

Coach Bryant's doctor, Dr. William Hill, said that the pressures of coaching were really not a factor in his death. In fact, he said that much of the pressure he might have felt had been relieved by his retirement. For that much, I am thankful.

The university administration wanted to cancel classes the next day as a tribute to Coach Bryant. But Mrs. Bryant would have no part of it. She said that Coach Bryant would have wanted us in class. It didn't matter much either way. Nobody attended class anyway.

The team met with Coach Goostree in the dorm annex the following day. It was there that we learned about all the plans for the memorial services and funeral. It was something nobody wanted to hear, but everyone knew they must. As the meeting adjourned, Coach Goostree asked Tommy Wilcox, Mike Mc-Queen, Darryl White, Paul Fields, Jeremiah Castille, Jerrill Sprinkle and Walter Lewis to stay a while longer. As it turned out, these people would be the pallbearers at the funeral. Eddie Lowe was also named, but couldn't make it. Paul Carruth was asked to take his place, and for awhile I envied him for that.

That night hundreds of people attended a memorial service in Memorial Coliseum. Everyone stood quietly as Mrs. Bryant and other members of the Bryant family walked into the auditorium. Evengelist Billy Graham offered his condolences in a telegram, and Steadman Shealy delivered a nice eulogy.

"He was a winner here on earth and I am convinced now that he is a winner with God," Steadman said. ". . .we thank you that we can know and believe that Coach Bryant went out a winner."

The funeral was on Friday. Five Greyhound buses picked the team up in front of Bryant Hall and carried us to the First United Methodist Church on Greensboro Avenue.

The church was far too small for a funeral of this magnitude. Only family members, friends, and former and present players were able to get inside the church. By the time the memorial services began, the church housed a veritable who's who of football. Lee Roy Jordan and John David Crow were there. So were Woody Hayes of Ohio State, Darrell Royal of Texas, Bobby Dodd of Georgia Tech, Frank Broyles of Arkansas, and Fran Curci, the former Kentucky coach. President Reagan sent George Allen as official representative from the White House. I saw Coach Perkins and his wife there, too. It was the first time I had seen him since early January. I'm sure there were others there that I didn't see. The press was not allowed inside the church at the family's request, staying outside along with thousands of others.

The coffin remained closed, a fact that both disturbed and relieved me. Draped over it was a blanket of red-and-white carnations.

Rev. Joe Elmore kept the eulogy simple:

> *Our thoughts today are of one person the Lord blessed and made a blessing. We give thanks to God for Paul Bryant!*
>
> *We give thanks to God for his long years of influence on young people, challenging them to excellence, discipline, confidence, and hard work.*
>
> *We give thanks to God for his love of life, his caring, his down-to-earth goodness.*
>
> *We give thanks to God for his ability to teach and motivate people—to teach them the important lessons for life—that we must never get too proud to pray, that to be a man is a matter of character and class, that the number one goal in life is to be a human being.*
>
> *We give thanks to God for his personal strength in leading men, and the tenderness with which he could touch a child.*
>
> *We give thanks to God for His—the sentence is completed in a multitude of ways in your minds and hearts, and those millions of people near and far!*
>
> *We give thanks to God for Paul Bryant!*

Millions of people did come from near and far. Or, at least, it seemed like millions. The police estimated that 700,000 people had lined the streets of Tuscaloosa as the white hearse carrying Coach Bryant passed Bryant-Denny Stadium for the last time. From my seat on the bus, I saw many people holding signs that read, *"Goodbye, Bear. We love you."*

From the church, the funeral caravan of 5 team buses, 6 police cars, 14 motorcycle cops and more than 300 private cars headed for Elmwood Cemetery in Birmingham.

The trip to Birmingham from Tuscaloosa is one that we had made many times before when we had a game at Legion Field. Usually, this 55-mile trip takes no time at all. But on the day of the funeral, the trip seemed to take forever.

For two-and-one-half hours, we sat solemnly as the funeral procession crept slowly down Interstate 59. The sun beat down on the bus windows, burning through the glass until the bus became an oven on wheels. We sat there in our coats and ties as perspiration trickled down our faces. I thought I was going to pass out, but didn't. The only sounds you could hear were a few sniffles in the back of the bus, a muffled cough here and there, and the rhythmic cadence of television helicopters hovering overhead. The quietness was numbing.

Were it not for the hundreds of people we saw along the way, I'm not sure any of us would have made it the whole 55 miles. From the old lady sobbing on the roadside to the construction crew who held their hardhats over their hearts as the funeral procession passed, it was obvious that the common man had lost a not-so-common hero.

It was also obvious at the cemetery. Almost 10,000 people were waiting at the burial site when our bus rolled through the cemetery's iron gates at around 12:30. People covered acres of the cemetery, standing on tombstones, sitting in tree branches. Some wore suits, but most came dressed in 'Bama jackets or baseball caps. I had feared the funeral would become a circus, but it didn't happen. It was so quiet at times you could hear a pin drop.

Like the memorial service, the graveside service was kept simple. Scriptures were read and everyone repeated the 23rd Psalm and the Lord's Prayer in unison. Coach Bryant's name was mentioned only twice throughout the entire ceremony. A modest epitaph for a modest man.

As the funeral ended, I saw an elderly woman stoop to pluck a carnation from a funeral wreath. A Birmingham policeman reached to stop her.

"Please, officer," she begged, "I don't have anything to remember him by. Please let me have just one flower. Please?"

The policeman sighed and then turned away. I walked back

to the bus crying.

Since his death, everyone has been trying to honor Coach Bryant in their own special ways. The Alabama and Arkansas state legislatures passed resolutions, others kicked around the idea of renaming Legion Field after him, and there was a moment of silence for him before the Super Bowl game between Washington and Miami. Still others tried to have the Talladega National Forest renamed, and a special record is still receiving air play on several radio stations around the state.

Another rumor that we would be playing Notre Dame in a special football game commemorating him had the whole team excited for awhile. Alabama has never beaten Notre Dame, but the chance to play them as a memorial to Coach Bryant had everyone fired up. Everyone that is except Perkins, who was against the idea. Somebody, I forgot who, asked him if he would play it, and he said he didn't want to start his first season with such a big game. That really ticked off Ricky Moore.

"I can't believe it," Ricky said after hearing the news. "We finally get another chance to play Notre Dame, and Perkins won't do it. He doesn't have much faith in us, does he?"

Several days ago, the university announced it would build an $11 million museum and convention center to be named "Paul W. Bryant Alumni/Continuing Education Center and Museum." Actually, this is a project that Coach Bryant had started last year after his 315th career win against Auburn. He said he wanted to do it, not because he wanted to be remembered, but because he wanted to honor the players who helped him win those 315 games.

I often got the feeling that he cared more about us than he did winning. Why else would he read us poems or clippings from Ann Landers' columns if it were not because he thought they would make us better people?

In my scrapbook back home, there are a couple of clippings of some things Coach Bryant said to the press when they began hounding him about going after Alonzo Stagg's record. I've almost memorized them—"If there's got to be a winningest coach in history," he had said, "it might as well be me." But then, in almost the same breath, he said, "In my lifetime, I may have put too much emphasis on winning because here I am—an old man— and the only fun I've had is winning and that's ridiculous. In 30 minutes it's over, and I'm looking forward to the next game."

I guess it's a lot like President Reagan said the day Coach Bryant died—"'Bear' Bryant gave his country the gift of a life unsurpassed."

And Coach Bryant kept giving even in death. Three months before he died, he had willed his eyes to an eye bank so that some sightless person could see. His wish was carried out.

He gave in other ways, too. He gave hope to those who had none.

I remember listening to his radio call-in show "Bearline," one night when I heard this young boy call in.

"Coach Bryant," the boy began, "I have a problem. I play peewee football, and everybody I have to block and tackle is about a foot taller than me and 50 pounds heavier. What can I do?"

"First, son," Coach Bryant answered, "let me tell you that you do have a problem. If I were you, I would mind my parents, study hard to get smarter, eat the right kinds of food, and pray for the Good Lord to make me stronger.

"As for now, son, stay down around their feet. No matter how big or how good a player is, you can stop him if you get to his feet."

Then, of course, there were the calls from middle-aged men who telephoned just to second-guess Coach Bryant's coaching in the previous game.

"Why did you run to the short side of the field when you had all that room over on the other side?" the Monday morning quarterback will ask.

"Because," Coach Bryant would say, "I was trying to win!"

But it was the calls from children that he enjoyed the most. He would always take more time with the children, and when he spoke, you could almost hear the laughter in his voice. My favorite call was one from a little boy who must've been around 5 years old.

"Coach Bryant?" the boy asked timidly.

"Yes?"

"I just wanted to talk to you."

"Good, because I want to talk to you. Your call flatters me."

They talked on for awhile with the conversation ending something like this:

"I love you, Coach Bryant."

"I love you, too, son."

"I want to play for you, Coach Bryant."

"You'd better hurry."

The trouble with talking about all these things that Coach Bryant has done and how people loved him is that it sound as if I'm trying to deify him. He wasn't a saint, of course—he was only human. Yes, he was given to occasional outbursts of profanity. And, yes, he didn't mind a good, stiff drink at times. As minor as these flaws may be, Coach Bryant was trying hard to overcome them. Steadman Shealy told me a few days after the funeral that Coach Bryant would often ask him to pray with him.

"As big and powerful a man as he was," Steadman said, "he never was too proud to get on his knees and pray."

Some people say that it wasn't fair that Coach Bryant should die so quickly after his retirement, that he should have been permitted to live at least awhile longer so that he may have enjoyed life. Pardon me for disagreeing, but if anyone knew how to get the most out of life and living, it was Coach Bryant.

He taught us how to gain victory and he taught us how to accept defeat. But more than anything, he taught us how to live.

There is a clipping of a poem stuck to the mirror in my dorm room. It was written by W. Heartsill Wilson, and it was one of Coach Bryant's favorite "ditties." I read it every day.

It goes like this:

> *This is the beginning of a new day*
> *God has given me this day to use as I will!*
> *I can waste it, or use it for good*
> *Because I am exchanging a day of my life for it*
>
> *When tomorrow comes,*
> *This day will be gone forever,*
> *Leaving something in its place*
> *I have traded for it*
> *I want it to be gain, not loss. . .*

I'll be danged if that ain't true.

PART VI

Hope Springs Eternal

February 17, 1983
Bryant Hall

It's recruiting time—do you know where your children are?

Normally, players don't pay much attention to the recruiting wars. Most could care less. Some fans are forever asking us questions about prospective recruits.

"Where do you stand with this big tackle out of Birmingham?" they'll ask.

And when we say, "I don't know," they think we're hiding something from them. But really it's because we honestly don't know or don't care.

I will have to admit, though, that we're all keeping a little closer tabs on Alabama's recruiting this year. We all want to see what kind of recruiter Perkins and the new assistants are going to be. After all that was one reason Coach Bryant decided to retire.

Many fans like to measure our recruiting season against Auburn's. It's like a game in itself with the "winner" being the one which signs the most blue chip prospects. Of course, most people in Tuscaloosa feel we're winning this year's recruiting race.

And, of course, each new recruiting season brings new rumors of recruiting violations. A popular line of thinking this year is that Ray Perkins had better be "careful" because Coach

Bryant isn't here to protect him from the NCAA. I have no doubt that the NCAA steered clear of Alabama when Coach Bryant was here, but I think that was more out of respect than intimidation.

Alabama has never been found guilty of breaking recruiting rules simply because it doesn't have to break them. Good players are going to come to Alabama because they want to be a part of the winning tradition.

When I was in high school, Alabama and Florida State were the only schools that showed any real interest in me. Other schools scouted me, some requested game films, and I was on every mailing list from Troy State to Nebraska. But there was never anything substantial from any of them. Even Troy State said it *might* offer me a scholarship.

Paul Carruth, on the other hand, could have gone to just about any major college he wanted. He could have gone to any of the three Mississippi schools, Florida, Tennessee, UCLA, LSU— just name it. He initially planned to sign with LSU, but on the morning that head coach Bo Rein was supposed to visit him, Rein's airplane disappeared over the Atlantic Ocean and he was never heard from again. After that happened, Paul verbally committed to Tennessee and then changed his mind. He was the next to the last player to sign with Alabama in February of 1981. And after he signed, his father told him that there were several schools who were willing to pay handsomely for him to sign on the dotted line.

An alumnus from one Southeastern Conference school pulled $10,000 in cash from his wallet and told Paul's dad, "it's yours if you'll get Paul to sign with us."

Paul's dad told the man what he could do with his money in no uncertain terms.

"Look," the man said, "just keep the money and think about it. I've done the same thing for another player from Mississippi and he changed his mind and went somewhere else. I gambled and I lost, but I let the kid keep the money. That's business."

But Paul's dad became so mad that he threw the guy out on his butt.

"Where is that guy now?" I asked Paul.

"In prison," Paul replied.

"In prison? What for?"

"Extortion, I think."

So, you can see that there are plenty of people out there willing to stoop to any level just to get a good player to sign with their school. And usually, it's the rich alumni who are the first to break the recruiting rules.

Florida is in hot water right now with the NCAA over alleged recruiting violations. NCAA officials have been investigating Florida for almost a year now, and instead of slowing down the inquiry seems to be only picking up steam.

Hardly a year goes by around here that NCAA enforcement officers don't visit our campus and ask some of our players about Florida recruiters or alumni. The NCAA once interrogated Jesse Bendross and Steve Booker about Florida.

As nosey as I am, I asked Jesse what they wanted to know about Florida. He wouldn't tell me.

So I asked, "What did you tell them?"

"Evverryy-thing!" Jesse said. "Those NCAA guys are just like FBI agents—they scared the heck out of me."

February 18

The hot topic of today is Herschel Walker. Reports out of Atlanta and Chicago say that Herschel has signed a multi-million dollar deal with the New Jersey Generals of the USFL. Herschel denies it.

Georgia coach Vince Dooley says that "the whole thing is underhanded, not above board, under-the-table type of dealing." In other words, he's mad.

And Herschel says, "In my heart and soul, I want to finish college and get my degree, and I think that's what I'm going to do."

If his heart and soul say "stay," I wonder what his pocketbook says?

February 23

Nasty rumor going around here today that we will be having a curfew during the spring. I hope it's only a rumor.

I was sitting in the dining room with Dante Bramblett and Scott McRae when The Governor walked up to our table.

"Yeah, you boys will have to start coming in sooner when spring practice starts," he said.

"What do you mean?" I asked. "We're not going to have curfew during the spring, too, are we?"

"It's not certain yet," he said, "but it looks that way."

Dante, Scott and I all agreed that that was ridiculous.

February 24

Herschel Walker made it official today. He signed a three-year, $5-million contract with the USFL's New Jersey Generals.

Herschel read a prepared statement in the signing ceremonies that could almost make you feel sorry for a man earning $5 million. He said he made a mistake in denying that he had signed a contract, and he apologized to Vince Dooley, the University of Georgia and all of his friends. He was near tears when he asked that they "forgive" him.

Coach Dooley said that Herschel "got too close to the fire and got burned." If $5 million is getting burned, I wouldn't mind being scorched just a little.

February 25

Just because it is the "off season" doesn't mean that we can sit around and get fat and lazy. In fact, some days during the off season are harder than any practice will ever be.

One of those days is today—Friday.

Friday is the day we go on Death Row, a special weekly workout that Coach Al Miller has devised for us.

Death Row is over with quickly; it takes only 20 to 25 minutes, but is far from painless. It is the hardest, most strenuous workout you'll ever get in your life. I have even seen players actually throw up after going through Death Row.

The workout consists of 10 exercise stations, from bench press to squats, and the player and a partner are supposed to go through each station as quickly as possible. Say you begin with the bench press—you would lie there pushing weights as hard and as fast as you can for 20 seconds, rest 10 seconds, push 20 seconds, rest 10, and so on. After a minute or so, your partner takes over and you rest while watching him. A small air horn sounds when it's time to move to the next station, and you begin all over again with the next exercise. The horn blows again and you move on to the next station. Over and over again. By the time you are finished with the whole routine, you are ready to drop dead.

Luckily for us, Friday comes only once a week. But in the meantime, Coach Miller is finding other fun things for us to do. He is in charge during the off season, and he takes his job seriously. Very seriously.

Since late January, Coach Miller has had us all on a tailored weight program designed to make us stronger for whatever position we play.

On Monday, it's power work—stuff like squats, deadlifts and snatches. On Tuesday, it's running—up and down the track stadium bleachers if it's warm outside, up and down the Coliseum bleachers if it's cold outside. Wednesdays are reserved for isolation workouts, such as curls, hamstring curls, leg extensions and vertical jumps. On Thursdays, it's more running. And Friday, of course, is Death Row.

Somehow, Coach Miller has managed to remain popular with the players through all this. Everyone knows that his workouts will make them better in the fall, but he is always challenging you to do a little extra. And he's always coming up with something new.

Right now, he has come up with the idea of holding a Super Stars decathlon on March 9 and 10. He says he will award so many points for each event, and it will take 950 points to make "Super Star" status. He insists that it will be fun. I doubt it. But it will break up the monotony around here.

February 27

Mike Adcock, Randy Edwards and I drove out to visit with Mrs. Bryant today. We hadn't seen her since the funeral. But we probably should have waited longer—she broke down and cried twice. I guess seeing us reminded her again that Coach Bryant is gone forever. It caused some pretty awkward moments.

She said people had been real nice to her during the past few weeks and showed us a guest bedroom filled with boxes and boxes of cards and letters she had received from fans. The boxes literally reached the ceiling.

"I don't know how I'm going to do it," she said, "but I'm going to try to answer every one of them."

She was also anxious to know how we were getting along with Coach Perkins. But because we hardly ever see him, we didn't know how to answer.

"Uh," I stuttered, "I think we'll like him."

"Well," she said, "Ray is not as tough as he thinks he is. He's a good ol' boy, though. Paul really liked him.

"He's so sweet. . .a lot of Paul's belongings are still in his office, and I've been so busy that I haven't been able to get up there and get them out of Ray's way. But he told me, 'That's OK. Don't you worry about it. You take all the time you want.' I thought that was real nice of him. I think you'll like Ray once you get to know him better."

Mrs. Bryant is such a wonderful conversationalist that we talked for an hour about everything under the sun. She is also a very warm person, and the whole team loves her. She has become a second mother to us all.

Listening to her talk, I found myself remembering how she sometimes would ride the team buses with us to the stadium. Everyone wanted to ride on the same bus she rode because that bus was always more fun, looser than the others. And riding with her made you feel very, very special.

Coach Perkins has changed his mind about becoming athletic director. Two weeks ago, he said the job was too much for one man to handle; today, he says he's the best man for the job.

The newspaper quotes him as saying "a lot has changed since that time." I'll have to agree with that—much has changed. And when you consider some of the public in-house battles that have plagued LSU, Auburn and other schools that had an athletic director and head football coach going head to head, it probably is best that Perkins be athletic director, too. It will give him more freedom to do the things he needs.

Maybe that ringing endorsement from Mrs. Bryant is softening me up some, huh?

Looks as if we're going to have to start spring practice without Ray Perkins.

Except for an occasional chance meeting, you hardly ever see Perkins around. And we *still* haven't received the first word on what this new pro-set offense is going to be like.

Time is running out. Spring practice should be starting up soon, and a lot of players have gotten tired of waiting.

I saw Walter Lewis and Paul Fields out on the practice field this afternoon, throwing the ball around. Linnie Patrick and Joe Carter were out there, too, working on catching the ball. They must be expecting a lot of passes to be thrown out of the backfield. Dante Bramblett was out there running wind sprints.

Watching these guys out there working out on their own makes me feel almost guilty, but only almost. I believe it is possible to overdo things. During my freshman and sophomore years, I made the mistake of working too much. I got so wrapped up in counting my steps on pass routes, dragging my foot and tucking in the ball that I forgot the most important element-catching the ball. I've since learned that you can't worry about those things. They have to come to you naturally or they're no good.

So, I'll wait. When the coaches are ready, I'll be ready.

March 6

Well, I thought I'd be ready.

Tonight, Coach Rockey Felker handed out the new playbooks, and I mean play*books*. Unlike the three or four new mimeographed sheets we used to get from Coach Bryant, these new playbooks are at least a half-inch thick and filled with hundreds of plays and formations. I wasn't prepared for this.

"Say you're ready to start learning a new offense, huh?" Felker said with a big mischievous grin.

I felt myself blushing. I wondered if he knew I had been complaining.

"Er uh, yes sir, Coach," I said. "I'm ready."

"That's good," he said, "because you've got a lot of learning to do. I know you can do it. I saw you and Jesse play against Penn State last year, and I know you can do the job. You have all the basic tools—you just need a little polishing.

"Study these new routes and formations until you can run 'em in your sleep. We'll be taking up the playbooks in two weeks or so, and we'll get down to business and start practice about March 21."

March 21? That doesn't leave much time.

I hurried back to my room and began thumbing through the playbook. I couldn't believe my eyes. Everything had been changed—the huddle, the formations, the terminology. And you can forget about that aerial circus everyone is expecting. It's not going to happen.

They even changed the name of my position. When my position was diagrammed out of the wishbone, I was known as the "Y" receiver. Now, I'm "X", Jesse is "Z", and the tight end is "Y." It's going to be tough to break that old habit.

We have more than 100 complex new formations to learn, stuff I've never even heard of. The wishbone was so simple—you either went right or you went left. The pro-set does the same thing, but you have a hundred different ways of getting there. I don't know if I'm ever going to learn all this.

Then there is the matter of reading defenses. I've never read a defense in my life, and I don't relish the idea of starting now. I'd rather just worry about running my route the way I did in the wishbone. But now I've got to check to see if a blitz is on. And if it is, I may have to change my route to a quick 5-yard out pattern so Walter can hit me. But then, there are other times when I won't have to change my route when the blitz is on. The playbook calls this "sight adjustment." I call it confusing.

Some changes I do like. One of these is a new V-shaped huddle called the "victory huddle." In this huddle, the quarterback steps back into the point of the "V" with running backs and linemen lining up on either side of him and the receivers on the end. Everyone is able to see the quarterback in this formation and it helps reduce confusion. The old huddle we used was nothing more than a circle. The center would start the circle with his back to the defense. He was then flanked on either side by the tackles, the guards, and running backs. The quarterback would close the circle by standing directly across from the center. The receivers stood on outside of the circle. I hated the old huddle because it usually meant that I'd have to tiptoe between Steve Mott and

Mike Adcock just so I could see into the huddle. I took a lot of teasing about that.

Another change I like is that I will now start a play from a standing position as opposed to the old three-point stance. The old stance was not only uncomfortable because you had to cock your head sideways to see the quarterback, but it left you vulnerable to defensive backs. This was a very bad position to be in during "bump" coverage because a fast defensive back could rush in and push your head into the ground before you knew what was happening. By starting from a standing position, you can improve your takeoff and elude defensive backs with a head fake and sharp turn, a move the playbook calls the "jab-go" move.

Another plus was finding out that Coach Felker would be handling the receivers instead of Coach Rader. Felker seems loose and laughs and smiles a lot—always a good sign. At least, I don't think he'll be having us do grass drills after practice.

That's about it for now; I've got a lot of studying to do.

March 7

I feel like an idiot.

Going through the playbook last night I noticed that the "x" receiver (me) routes all seemed to go 15 yards downfield and then cut inside. Since this is the kind of route that usually turns wide receivers into chopped liver, I was naturally concerned. Not only that, but there hardly seemed to be any plays where I could go deep on.

I was so worried about this that I went to Coach Felker about it.

"What's the deal with this?" I asked. "This says I'm always lined up on the right side, and all the routes are in-routes. My best route used to be going deep. Will I never go deep anymore?

I was panicking, but Coach Felker was amused. He started laughing at me.

"Just because the playbook shows you lining up on the right side all the time doesn't mean that we'll always run it from that side," he said and laughed. "That play can go to the left, too. Everything would be the same, but reversed."

"I wouldn't be so worried about that in-route," he went on. "That play is going to be our best third-and-long play.

"Well," I said, "it sure looks like you are going to be depending on me on a lot of third-down situations."

"We are," he said, "but that doesn't mean we won't be throwing to you deep. You'll get some long passes, too."

So it appears my fear was unfounded. But I still don't like that "in" route.

March 8

Hallelujah! there won't be a spring curfew. That's the best news I've had in a long time.

We got the word Sunday night in a meeting with Coach Perkins to discuss the "new rules to live by." But it wasn't the only good word.

Coach Perkins said that he does not condone drinking, but he isn't going to babysit us, either.

"I know about a few of the bars here," he said. "And I've heard about the place where most of you go. I'm not going to tell you not to go there, but if you do, I expect you to show your class wherever you go.

"Don't show your ass. Don't get into trouble. And don't be calling me at four in the morning to tell me you're in jail. If you get into trouble anywhere, you'll be in trouble with me."

Not that it matters, but that's quite a turnaround from Coach Bryant's policy. With Coach Bryant, you were immediately in trouble if he or an assistant coach saw you at a nightclub. Of course, players went out anyway but they were always nervous about it and always on the lookout.

Randy Edwards is excited about growing a beard now that Coach Perkins has said it's OK "as long as it's neat and not scraggly." There was no way Coach Bryant would've let you grow a beard. Of course, Perkins is still concerned about our appearance. He says that no cut-off or sleeveless T-shirts will be allowed in the cafeteria.

Those are the unwritten rules. The six-page guideline of dormitory rules he passed out was virtually unchanged. The rules really aren't *that* bad and are really nothing more than common sense—no pets, except fish, allowed, no loud noise or horseplay, female guests not allowed on second and third floors at any time, keep your room neat, and so on.

Like I said before, they're just common sense rules. But common sense does not always prevail in a college dormitory. One of my favorite pastimes is throwing a box of soap suds out of Mike Adcock's dorm window and into the water fountain below. And when I was a freshman, I found it too inconvenient to walk 50 yards down the hallway to use the restroom, so I simply raised a window and let it fly. That window is what we call the "freshman bathroom."

Many rules are broken not out of spite, but out of boredom—like the time Rocky Colburn tape recorded the sound of his roommate sitting on the toilet. Rocky then played the tape back full blast—from grunt to sigh to flush.

Still, it must be pretty tame now compared to previous years. One of the tales still told around here is the time when Steve Whitman bought a thousand live crickets from a bait shop and turned them loose in someone's room. And players still talk about the time Rich Wingo set a fraternity's homecoming float on fire.

Ah, yes, boys will be boys. . .

Tomorrow is the big day for Coach Al Miller's first annual "Super Stars" competition. I wonder what kind of surprises he has in store for us?

March 9

My thigh muscles are in knots, my calves are sore, and I feel like an Army platoon has just ran across my stomach. But that's OK—I'm on my way to becoming a "Super Star."

Coach Miller's "Super Stars" competiton was just as I thought it would be—tough. Today, I competed in box jumps, the shuttle run, the vertical jump, sit-ups, and dips. Tomorrow, it's the back squat, bench press, maze run and two 440 runs. I don't know if I'll live through it.

I did better than I expected today. I did 31 box jumps in 30 seconds, I ran the 20-yard shuttle run in 18.1 seconds, I reached 33 and 3/4 inches on the vertical jump, and did 67 sit-ups in 60 seconds and 32 dips.

The price of glory doesn't come cheap.

March 10

Have you ever noticed how most people never achieve fame until they're dead? I have.

I thought about that real hard today while I was lying on the training room table, nearly unconcious after running two 440-yard dashes in a freak snowstorm. For a minute there, I thought I was going to throw up snowballs.

But I'm not complaining. Super stars don't complain. And I'm a bona fide Al Miller "Super Star." He says he's going to hang my picture on the wall of the weight room to prove it.

As a matter of fact, I am the only player on the whole team to make "Super Star" status. I collected the prescribed 950 points out of the possible 1,000, but I paid dearly for it.

I began with the squats and pressed 175 pounds 30 times. After that, I bench pressed my weight (167) 18 times. Then I moved outside where it was snowing to run my 440s. I ran the first one in 54 seconds, rested two minutes, and ran the second one in 62 seconds. By that time, I was ready to pass out. I went into the training room to die, but Coach Miller wouldn't let me. Instead, he called me in for my maze run. I finished that with the best time of anybody—21.4 seconds.

And what do I get for this near attempt at suicide?

That's right—a pat on the back and my picture on the wall of the training room.

March 15

They took down Coach Bryant's tower today and hauled it away. I'm just glad I didn't see them do it.

I was driving along in my car when I heard about it on the radio. I wasn't sure I had heard correctly, so I wheeled the car around and drove by Thomas Field to see for myself. Sure enough, the tower was gone. In its place was a small mound of red dirt. I wanted to cry.

My first reaction was something like, "Oh, no, how could Perkins do this?" To me, it was like desecrating a national monument. Then, I decided it was probably for the best. Had the tower remained, we would have all felt that Coach Bryant was watching over our shoulders.

I guess Coach Bryant really is gone now. There's no turning back.

March 16

Everybody is staying busy studying the new playbooks, and each day brings a new question about it.

But studying is a lonely business. You can't ask a teammate how a certain play is to be run—he doesn't know himself. It's the blind leading the blind.

March 18

A few players are mad about Coach Perkins removing Coach Bryant's tower. Mike Adcock is not one of them.

"To me, the tower *was* Coach Bryant," Mike said "When I think of the tower, I don't want to think of anyone but Coach Bryant. Let Coach Perkins make his own memories. . ."

Death Row claimed one victim today. Al Blue quit.

Al, a senior defensive back from Maitland, Florida, was halfway finished (halfway started, depending on how you look at it) when he threw the weights down and his hands up.

"Shoot, man, I can't take this stuff no more," he said.

This, of course, infuriated Coach Miller.

"Get out of here then!" he shouted. "We're not going to put up with any quitters. Coach Perkins doesn't want anybody quitting on him during a game, so you might as well quit now. Go on! Just get on out of here!"

Al wiped his face with a towel and walked out without saying a word to anyone.

March 20

The depth chart lists me at first team offense and I'll be wearing a red jersey in practice tomorrow, but Coach Perkins says that doesn't mean a thing.

"Right now, nobody is first team," he told us in a meeting today. "We've got the lineups set up the way they are now, but that's just because that's how it was last year. But I can tell you right now, my eyes are wide open."

What all of this means is that everybody will be starting out as equals. Nobody is guaranteed a starting job.

To emphasize this point, Coach Perkins has abolished our old system of identifying different units by jersey colors. In the past, the first team offense wore red, the first team defense wore white, the second team offense wore green, the second team defense wore blue, and all units below that wore yellow or orange.

Now, there will be only four jersey colors in practice—red for offense, white for defense, blue for quarterbacks, and yellow for injured players.

"I don't want to distinguish anybody as being on a lower level," Perkins said. "After all, we are all on the same team."

I suppose this is good in a way. I remember what I went through my freshman year. I wore the green jersey only one season, but it seemed like an eternity. If you never moved up, you lost confidence. By the same token, seeing those red jerseys gave you something to shoot for. And when you put on that red jersey you felt as if you owned the world.

Old habits die hard, though. We will still have names for the different units. The first team offense will still be called Reds. The first team defense will still be called Head Hunters. The second team offense will still be called Jets. The second team defense will still be called "H" (figure that one out). And the third team offense and defense will still be called Colors.

Danny Holcombe was a perennial Jet. Danny was a center (since graduated) who was never able to move up to the Red team, but he took it in stride. In fact, he was proud of his role in preparing the first team defense for the next game.

"It takes Jet pride to play this game," he'd say.

March 21

Coach Perkins called off practice today because of rain and cold. Paul Carruth was really disappointed about the delay. He is anxious to start learning this new offense.

Paul also has a lot to prove, not just to the new coaches, but to the other players and himself. In all the years he's been here, Paul has never finished a spring practice. He has always gotten hurt on the first day and had to sit out the rest of the spring.

With a little free time on my hands, I thought it might be interesting to give you an idea of what our roster looks like this year.

One highlight of an otherwise sub-par Alabama season was Coach Bryant's record-tying 314th win. We beat Penn State 31-16.

One of the advantages of being the home team is having a side-line air con-ditioner during those hot afternoon games.

This was my first start at Alabama. I had three catches for 100 yards and one touchdown. I finally got to prove myself to Coach Bryant.

At low tide. . .Coach Bryant, Coach Moore, Steadman Shealy, and myself mirror the frustration of an 8-4 season.

Alabama receivers have a great tradition to uphold. Do you recognize these Crimson Tide stars?

Hint: They both became coaches for the same university.

The changing of the guard. With the grace befitting a legend, Coach Bryant steps down.

It was a sad time for both players and fans. Coach Perkins and his wife Carolyn led the team out of the funeral service (left). The procession took Coach Bryant on one last trip past the University of Alabama landmarks that meant so much to him, and ended up at Elmwood Cemetery where thousands of fans said goodbye (above).

Why do receivers like to run deep rather than go across
the middle, you ask?. . .

...The end result can be dramatically different.

I didn't take ballet lessons like Lynn Swann, but scoring this touchdown against Tennessee really made me feel like dancing.

It doesn't matter what league you're in, sometimes they aren't thrown right where you want 'em. So you just go get 'em.

The practices under Coach Perkins were much different. The tower was gone. Just like Coach Bryant in his younger days, Coach Perkins stays in the thick of the action. (That's a not-so-flattering view of my roomie, Paul Carruth, in front of Coach Perkins.

That "icy stare" was even more intense when the first whistle blew for each game.

Thanks to "Little Joe" Henley all my superstitions were complied with. Five minutes before game time he put the war paint under my eyes to prevent glare.

The score was 40-0 over Ole Miss, so I decided to doctor my ankle and get ready for next week.

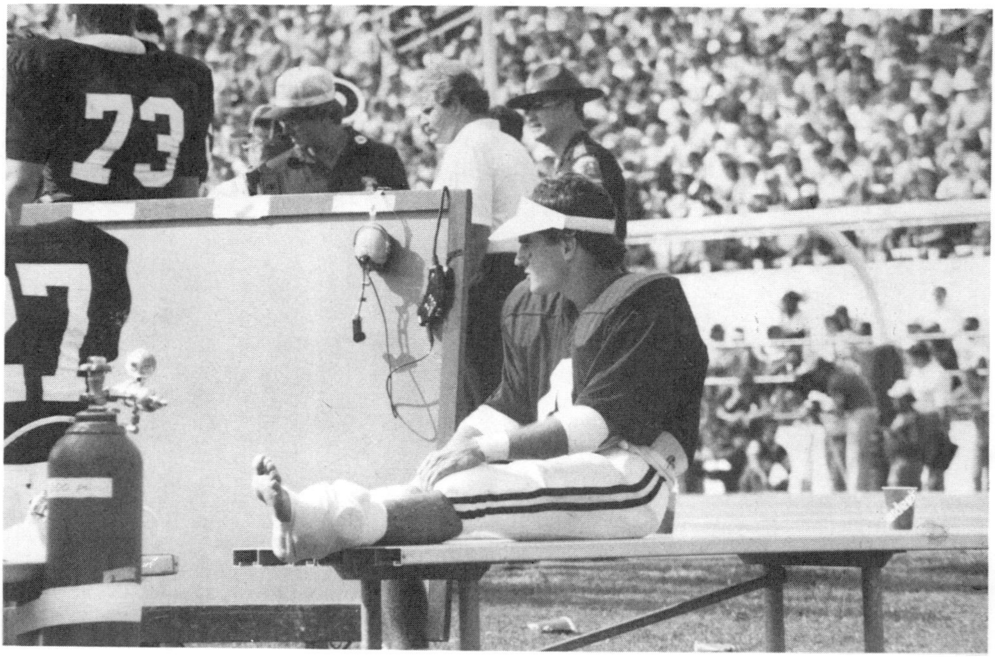

This was my last game—my last touchdown—my last chance to celebrate with my teammates. Wes Neighbors (54), Ricky Moore (26), and Thornton Chandler (81) help me celebrate our 28-7 Sun Bowl win over 4th ranked SMU.

SUCCESS

Success is finishing what you planned
   from the beginning of eagerness;
To dream of the rewards
   and of the happiness.

Along the tough road to success,
   your confidence can grow thin,
And before you know what is happening
   your eagerness can blow in the wind.

But a champion never quits
   and lets nothing in his way.
Yes, nothing can stop him
   Not even disappointment from a bad day.

Once you surpass the pain
   your confidence shoots high,
There is a smile on your face
   and you know exactly why.

You have accomplished your goal
   without being a sinner.
There is no better feeling
   than to know you are a WINNER!

                    Joey Jones

It goes without saying that offense will be our strong suit. Returning starters include Jesse Bendross at flanker, Doug Vickers at strong tackle, Mike Adcock at quick guard, Ricky Moore at fullback, Paul Carruth at halfback, Walter Lewis at quarterback, Jay Grogan at tight end, and of course, myself at split end. Gone are offensive starters fullback Jeff Fagan, guard Gary Bramblett, tackle Joe Beazley, and our "warped" game captain, Steve Mott.

Defensively, we could be hurting. Randy Edwards will be back at tackle and Mike Rodriguez will be at nose guard, but after that, we start hurting. We've lost both starting defensive ends in Mike Pitts and Russ Woods, and Jackie Cline is now playing tackle for the Birmingham Stallions.

I'm afraid our secondary is going to be our weakest area. We've lost two all-American defensive backs in Jeremiah Castille and Tommy Wilcox and two good linebackers in Eddie Lowe and Robbie Jones. That leaves Stan Gay at right cornerback as the only true starter returning to the secondary, along with part-time starter Rocky Colburn at strong safety.

March 22

I see now why Coach Perkins was waiting until tomorrow to start spring practice—he wanted to be athletic director on the day practice began.

He got what he wanted today. He is now head coach and athletic director. The only person he has to answer to now is the University president, Dr. Joab Thomas.

While this is probably for the best, I can't help thinking about Coach Sam Bailey. Coach Bailey has been assistant athletic director for so long that he even looks like Coach Bryant. He wanted the athletic director's job, too. Maybe he will be able to keep his old job anyway.

Seems like every time I pick up a newspaper these days, some sportswriter is saying Walter, Jesse and I are the reason Coach Perkins is changing to a pro-set offense.

This is all very flattering, but it worries me. What if we *don't* have a good year?

March 23

Spring practice. Day One.

I made a half-dozen great catches today and I ran one bad route. Which do you think Coach Perkins noticed? You guessed it.

I was working on that 15-yard in route that I detest so much when I heard Perkins yelling, "No! No! That not how you do it!"

I was rounding off the route too much, not cutting back in as sharply as I was supposed to. He wanted me to drag and push the defensive back's shoulder.

"Look," he said in a voice loud enough for everyone to hear, "you be a defensive back. I want to run a route, all right?"

Then, he began walking through the route I had run, talking as he moved along.

"If I round it in like this, I don't ever get your shoulders turned in, do I?

"Uh, no sir," I mumbled.

"Huh?!"

"No sir, Coach."

Then, he began walking through the route again. Only this time, he darted as he reached me and then turned back to the inside of the field sharply.

"But if I round it off right here," he said, planting his foot into the turf, "and give a sharp jump toward your shoulders, you have to move. Don't you?"

"Yes, sir."

"And you've got to respect that move, don't you?"

"Yes, sir."

"The defensive back has got to turn with that move," he went on. "You've got to cut off his inside shoulder. You've got to give a burst right there at the end to get him turned around.

"You're never going to be able to do anything if you don't get him out of the backfield and turned around. If you don't do that, you're not going to be an effective receiver."

"That," he said, "is the key to getting open."

He said it sarcastically, and he had that glare in his eyes that I hate and that half smile, half sneer on his face. I wanted to dig a hole and hide.

He knew I didn't know that route, but here I was getting chewed out on my first day of practice. So much for first impressions, huh?

Impressions don't mean much anyway. I thought Coach Felker was going to be an easy-going, laid-back coach who smiles all the time. Boy, was I ever wrong.

Coach Felker doesn't smile half as much on the football field, and he darn near ran us to death. He had us running routes, diving for low balls, jumping for high balls, and running cone drills. As soon as one drill was over, it was "Hustle! Hustle!" to the next one.

Jesse Bendross plopped down on the bench in the locker room after practice and groaned, "Man, I ain't never run so much in my whole life!"

Paul Carruth said that "Coach Arians would jump down your throat if you messed up, but not anything like Coach Henshaw does. He's going to take some getting used to."

My route running notwithstanding, I think it was a good practice all in all. Under Coach Bryant, our first day of practice would be in shorts and pads. But today, we came out in full gear and went full tilt with a lot of hitting. It was, "Damn the torpedoes, full speed ahead."

We practiced three hours in the cold and wind, but there were so many short, specialized drills that it passed by rather quickly.

Just the same, it felt strange holding spring practice without Coach Bryant watching us from his tower. As I was walking onto the field today, I overheard Craig Turner say, "Man, this field sure looks a lot bigger without Coach Bryant's tower there." He was right.

Mike Adcock said he was having trouble adapting to the new blocking techniques.

"The first time I messed up," Mike said, "I instinctively looked in the direction of the tower to see if Coach Bryant was watching me. I was relieved when I remembered he was gone."

Well, Paul Carruth made it through his first day of spring practice unscathed, It didn't go unnoticed, either.

On the chalkboard in the dressing room, someone has already started counting down the days of practice. And underneath that, Randy Edwards has begun adding up the days of practice that Paul Carruth gets through unhurt.

"Well, that's one day down and 19 to go for Paul Carruth," Randy announced as he made the first marking. "Now the question is, 'Can he make it two days in a row?'"

March 26

Each day we begin and end practice with something Coach Perkins calls a "pride drill." We gather around him and he yells, "Pride!" Then we respond with, "Pride!" We do this about three times before beginning or ending a practice.

Coach Perkins says he doesn't intend for this to be a "big hyped-up kind of thing."

"It's just a little reminder of the pride you take onto this field, and the pride you should carry with you when you leave the field."

I thought that was a nice touch.

My old social life is about dead now that spring practice is here. If we aren't practicing, we're having team meetings. I have just come from my fourth meeting of the day, and now I'm too tired to do anything else.

This many meetings is hard for us to take. Coach Bryant never had team meetings during the spring. The only time he would talk to us would be before and after practice, and then it was just for a few minutes.

Most players say they hate these meetings, but we all know it's necessary. How else are we going to learn this new offense?

We had another casualty today. Coach Perkins announced in the press that Chuck McCall, a junior middle guard from Montgomery, had quit the team to concentrate on his studies.

Rain wiped out practice yesterday and cut today's practice short. Coach Perkins says all the lightning made him nervous.

Mike McQueen saw it another way.

"If Coach Bryant were still here," he said, "he would've said, 'Rain? What rain?!' And it would've stopped immediately."

March 29

A player always likes to know where he stands with the coaches. One way I do this is by checking the *Tuscaloosa News* each day to see what Coach Perkins has to say about our last practice.

Coach Perkins said we did well in practice yesterday. I thought we stunk. Either he is trying to build up our confidence or he was at a different practice than I was. It wasn't like that with Coach Bryant. With him, if you were terrible, he said so.

I'm beginning to realize that precision is more important than ever in running pass routes. One step too many or one step not enough won't do. Coach Felker wants perfection—so do I.

Coach Perkins was to meet with the wide receivers, running backs and quarterbacks today to go over some of the plays. I got there about two minutes late. The door was already closed and I could hear Coach Perkins inside. Rather than interrupt, I waited outside the door.

Then I heard Coach Perkins say, "Did Joey Jones ever make it?"

That was my cue.

"Here I am, Coach!" I said, waving my hand as I popped into the room.

He glared at me with that look of his and said, "Well, better late than never I guess."

Once again, I felt like crawling in a hole.

After the meeting was over, I went up and apologized for being late.

"No, don't worry about it," he said. "If you're late, just come on in."

That floored me. If you were one second late for Coach Bryant's meetings, you had better not come in at all.

March 30

Whenever I start feeling sorry for myself because I've got so much to learn, I just have to look at Walter Lewis.

A split end has it bad, but a quarterback has it ten times worse. Not only does Walter have to learn what he has to do, but he also has to learn what everybody else must do.

I was always amazed at the way Walter handled the option plays in the wishbone, but that was nothing compared to what he's doing now. Now he is having to learn a hundred or so new formations, watch out for two receivers and a tight end, read every defensive coverage imaginable, call audibles at the line to adjust to different defenses, and a thousand other things. Figuring out which play will work best against a certain defense is not an easy thing to do. Think about that the next time you boo a quarterback.

Despite Walter's poor showing yesterday, the official progress report quoted Coach Perkins as saying Walter is "improving every day."

I'm sure Coach Perkins has heard about some of the things Walter has had to go through, being the first black to start at quarterback here. But Coach Perkins seems intent on letting Walter know he's behind him. And by publicly praising Walter in the press, he's letting the fans know that he's behind Walter 100 percent.

You know, I think I could get to like Coach Perkins.

April 1

My knee has been hurting like the devil. It feels like two bones in my knee cap are rubbing together. The faster I run, the harder they rub.

I'm scared to go to our trainer, Jim Goostree, with it. The first unwritten rule of spring training is, "Stay out of the training room." Players who have gone into that training room thinking they had only a minor injury have never been heard from again.

"Goose" hates injuries worse than Mr. Clean hates dirt. If you get hurt, he automatically assumes it's all your fault. Telling him that you are hurt is like telling him that he talks through his nose, which he does.

Last year I sprained my ankle and tried my darndest to hide it from "Goose." I had a bucket full of ice hidden in a corner of the training room and was soaking my foot when I saw him walk in.

I yanked my foot away, covered the bucket with a towel, and immediately began bouncing around on my sprained ankle. I was doing everything but somersaults on that sore ankle. I gave him the entire "See, I'm not hurt" routine. And the whole time, I kept my eye on "Goose."

As soon as he left the room, I sunk to the floor in pain. I embraced my sore ankle, apologized to it with tears in my eyes, and moaned, "Oohh, God, that hurts!"

April 2

In the locker room today, there was some grousing about Coach Henshaw's screaming tirades when Mal Moore's name came up.

"What about Coach Moore?" I asked

"He's the offensive coordinator at Notre Dame now," said Craig Turner.

"No kidding? When did that happen?"

"Last month."

Which reminds me. . .I talked with Coach Marks the other day. He is now a scout for the Denver Broncos. You just can't keep a good man down.

April 4

Sometimes I think it would be a good idea to field a team with one quarterback and ten running backs. We have enough good ones that we could do it.

Ricky Moore is having another good spring. He always does. Craig Turner, Joe Carter and my roomie are all looking good too. Even Linnie Patrick is having more good days than bad.

Chester Braggs is doing well at halfback, and Don Horstead, Mickey Guinyard and Chuck Fields are looking good at fullback.

But of them all, I have to say that Chuck Fields has made the greatest turn-around. A year ago, I would have bet that Chuck would never have made this team. He never seemed happy and was always complaining about one thing or another. But a couple of months ago, he started attending a lot of Fellowship of Christian Athletes meetings and turned his whole life around. He doesn't even seem like the same person off the field. And on the field, he'll get you a first down or he will die trying.

April 5

Hell has no fury like a frustrated coach.

Every man has his limit, and Coach Perkins reached his today. We held our second full-scale scrimmage this afternoon, and the defense drilled us. Afterwards, Coach Perkins chewed us up and spit us out.

"You have made no progress whatsoever from the first scrimmage!" he shouted. "You're supposed to be getting better! The defense *is* getting better, but the offense hasn't improved a bit. The defense dominated you! They killed you!"

He gave the defense all the credit, and us all the blame.

He let the defense shower and go home. We had to stay another 45 minutes.

April 6

I think yesterday's practice awakened us. The offense did much better today. We are finally realizing that we can't continue using the new offense as an excuse.

I let my guard down today, and Coach Perkins noticed I was limping.

"Is your knee hurting you?" he asked.

"Just a little," I lied.

"Have you hurt it before?"

"Yes, sir. I hurt it last year and it really hasn't been the same since."

"You'd better get it seen about."

"Yes, sir."

And I will—later.

No sooner had I walked off the field today than Coach Goostree cornered me.

"Why didn't you come to me about that knee?" he asked accusingly.

I knew right away that Coach Perkins had told him about it.

"Well, Coach," I said, "it really wasn't bothering me that bad."

"Well, get on in there and let's get some ice on it."

He was so nice about it, he surprised me. You get to be a senior and he isn't so bad.

One of our favorite leisure activities around here is teasing Steve Booker about his missing front tooth.

We call him "Snag," "Snaggle" or anything else that will get a rise out of him.

Today, while Booker was in the whirlpool soaking a pulled hamstring, Mike Adcock took a minute to examine Booker's locker.

"Hey! If you want to see something funny, come look at this!" Adcock said, laughing as he dangled Booker's mouthpiece in the air.

Everyone gathered around to see what Adcock was laughing about. It was Booker's mouthpiece—molded in the shape of his teeth and indented where his front tooth was missing.

Everyone was still laughing when Booker walked into the room.

"Hey, Snag!" someone shouted. "That's a cute little mouth-piece you've got there!"

"Yeah," someone else said, "ain't nobody gonna steal that one from you!"

Embarrased, Booker went on the offensive.

"Shut up!" he said "Ain't none of ya'll can say nothin' 'about me. Every one of ya'll got somethin' wrong with ya'll. I just happen to have a tooth wrong with me.

"I can find somethin' wrong with every one of ya'll real quick like. Anyone want to say somethin'?"

April 7

Two more walk-ons bit the dust today. As bad as it may

sound, quite frankly I'm glad they're gone.

We began spring training with about 20 receivers in all. Of all those, only Jesse Bendross, Joe Smith, Craige Florence and I are scholarship players. The rest are walk-ons, people who simply weren't good enough players to be offered a full athletic scholarship, or people who suddenly decided that it would be a "neat idea" to play college football.

Occasionally, a walk-on will surprise you. Ed Pugh, a walk on from Opelika, will probably see a lot of action on the specialty teams this fall,and he's running second team to Jesse right now. And there's a tall, lanky kid from New York, Billy Getchel, who is showing a lot of potential.

But as a rule, most walk-ons aren't very good and have no business being on a college football field. Most have a poor knowledge of the game or lack the basic physical skills needed to get the job done. After awhile, most will realize this and go back to their Sunday afternoon flag football games.

I do realize, however, that walk-ons have become a vital part of many football programs. Since colleges are limited on the number of scholarships they can legally offer, coaches have become more selective about who is given a scholarship. Sometimes, there are more good players around than there are scholarships. When that happens, a coach may invite a good prospect to "walk on." Eventually, that player could earn a scholarship.

That is why the coaches encourage us to help the walk-ons along by explaining things to them or by offering helpful hints. And besides, most walk-ons look up to the starters as if we are heroes or something.

So, when you see a walk-on make a so-so catch, you try to make it sound like the greatest catch you've ever seen.

"Man!" you'll say, "That was a bee-yoo-tiful catch!"

You can see their faces light up as they come back to the huddle. You've made their day.

April 12

This is the big week of the A-Day game. We picked the teams today and it will be the first offense and second defense against the first defense and second offense. I'll be on the Red team.

On paper, the White team looks as if they may have an edge

because of all their depth. Their offense can almost match up to ours, and they have a better defense. We'll just have to see how that goes Saturday.

I'm curious as to how the coaches are going to handle A-Day this year. I don't know if it will be a fun thing like it usually is, or if it will be a big pressurized scrimmage with the coaches screaming at us all day long. I guess I'll find out about that too.

April 13

With practices getting harder and longer, I am finding it harder to get out of bed. I lay in bed until 12:15 today and skipped all of my classes.

Finally, around 12:30, I went downstairs to the cafeteria to get something to eat. I saw Walter sitting at a table with Paul Fields, and I thought I would impress him by calling one of our more complicated plays with the hand signals.

"Hey, Walter!" I said. "Roger Flood Z Half Fly 122 X Q!"

I then furiously began tapping my head, shoulders, hips and thighs, while waving my arms around wildly. I must have looked like a contortionist because Walter laughed at me until he had tears in his eyes.

"No, No," he said, "it's like this. . ."

He went through the signals as if he had been weaned on them. I felt like a fool. I tucked my tail between my legs and sauntered off to eat my meal in peace—smart alecky quarterbacks!

Another tough practice today. My pass catching is much better now, and I'm beginning to get the hang of that 15-yard "in" route. Another week or so and I should have it down perfectly.

I'm also starting to see eye-to-eye with Coach Felker and Coach Perkins now. We seem to be building a pretty good player-coach relationship. Let's hope it continues.

The "Tough Hit of the Day Award" goes to Rodney Jarmon, who turned Jesse Bendross head over heels on an incomplete pass.

Said Jesse: "Where did he come from?!"

Said someone else: "Florence."

Footnote to a busy day: The University of Florida today

issued its third denial in two months that Charley Pell would resign as head coach. Hang in there, Charley.

April 13

One of the great success stories of the spring that isn't getting much attention in the press is Billy Getchel, the walk-on wide receiver from Upback, New York.

Billy, who has a very strong northern accent, tells me that he walked on here last year as a defensive back, but I don't remember him. He says he switched to wide receiver because he felt we lacked depth here.

"Look," he said, "I know I can't beat you and your podner (meaning Jesse) out, but I hope I can at least get in some playing time."

When I first met him, I thought, "Who is this guy? He can't be any good. He'll probably drop every pass that comes to him."

But as it turns out, Billy is a very good wide receiver. He knows how to get open, can catch the ball in a crowd, and runs solid routes.

The amazing thing is that Billy never even put on shoulder pads until he came to Alabama. In fact, the only football he had played until last year was an organized flag football league that played its games in the city streets.

Somehow the subject turned to street gangs, and I asked Billy if they had them where he lived.

"Plenty of them," he said. "One night I was walking down the street when I saw a black gang walking toward me with clubs and switchblades in their hands. I started looking for a place to run, but then I saw another street gang closing in from my right. I turned around and saw another Peurto Rican gang closing in with chains and sticks in their hands. That's when I realized it wasn't me they were after—they were about to have a fight over their turf."

"What did you do?" I asked.

"I ducked into a tenement house and watched them fight it out from the balcony."

April 14

Everybody loves a good fight. And in football, the next best thing is watching the linemen in one-on-one drills.

There is nothing quite as exciting as when Coach Tom Goode pits his offensive linemen against Coach Donahue's defensive linemen. When these giant-sized men go at one another, butting heads, pushing and shoving, it always draws a crowd.

Our drills are dull by comparison. We're over there running these little five-yard "out" patterns and making sure we get a toe down inside the boundary line, while the linemen are on the other side of the field waging head-to-gut combat. You can hear the grunting and the pads popping a half mile away.

And when two roommates, say Mike Adcock and Randy Edwards, go head-to-head, out goes the battle cry, "Roomies! Roomies!"

Theirs is a battle for self-pride. There's no glory involved. Oh, some sportswriter will do a story on them maybe once a year, but mostly they are ignored. They fight for self-satisfaction, knowing they whipped somebody, and they thrive on it.

Maybe it is cliche to say that football games are won or lost in the trenches, but it's the truth. I will always believe that.

Let's face it, I guess I'm just a closet lineman.

With Steve Mott lost to graduation, there has been a battle for starting center between Wes Neighbors and Mark Jackson. Only it hasn't been much of a battle.

Mark was the backup to Steve last season, but he's being pushed hard by Wes. Wes is a freshman redshirt from Huntsville whose father was an All-American linebacker here in the early 1960s. He was originally going to follow in his Dad's footsteps by being a linebacker, but he has moved over to center this spring. I think it was a good move. Wes was "built" for it—short and stocky with shoulders so broad that his shirt size is "Wide Load." He is quick, too. And because he is so short, he is able to fire off the line and cut defenders down at their knees, a maneuver commonly called "submarining."

If Wes keeps this up, poor Mark is going to need an awful lot of that Jet pride.

April 15

With the A-Day game coming up tomorrow, we took today off and I've enjoyed every minute of it.

Mom just got into town, and I took her out for a nice dinner. Afterwards, I carried her back to the hotel and we had a good talk. Willie Crabtree, a friend from Mobile, stopped by and we talked for awhile, too.

Tomorrow morning, I'll carry Mom and Willie to a big barbeque they're holding for the players and their families. I'll get there early so my food will have time to digest before the game.

But right now, I don't believe I could eat anything. I'm already getting butterflies about the game. There are an awful lot of people out there wondering what the heck is going to happen to Alabama football this season. They're wondering about the new offense, and they're wondering if Ray Perkins can carry on the tradition started by Coach Bryant. And I guess they're wondering about me, too. I feel I've proven myself to the coaches and to myself, but now I must face my biggest critics—the fans. If I go out and screw up just one day, the fans are going to think we haven't done anything all spring. We've just got to put on a good show.

April 17

It was a great fight, Mom, but we lost.

The White team beat us 14-11, and it would have been worse if I hadn't caught a 35-yard touchdown pass from Perry Cuda on the last play of the game.

About 23,000 people came to see our new pass-happy offense, and they certainly got their money's worth. A total of 81 passes were thrown and 37 were completed for 446 yards. I personally accounted for 173 of those yards on eight catches. I never thought I'd see that happen at Alabama.

It was far from perfect, however. I don't know why, but we made more mistakes than we made in our first scrimmage. We combined for six interceptions, 11 fumbles, and four missed field goals. I believe most of these mistakes can be corrected with time.

Still, this game was all in fun. Coach Perkins watched from the press box and turned the coaching over to the assistants.

Coach Donahue stood on the White team sideline, trying to out-guess us. We'd line up on the ball, and he would yell to the defense, "It's a run! Run! Run!" Then, we would pass and Steadman Shealy would yell across the field at Coach Donahue, "See, ol' man?! You ain't so smart after all!"

Rodney Jarmon hit me so hard on one pass that my helmet turned sideways and I laid on the field, staring out of my ear-hole. As I lifted myself off the ground, Roosevelt Hill was laughing and pointing at me.

"Hooo-ey!" Roosevelt said. "He killed you, man! He killed you!"

April 18

Who says you can't have your steak and eat it, too?

The losers had to serve the winners steak tonight. We put on our little aprons and worked in the kitchen, bringing out the food to members of the winning team. It was really embarrassing, but it did have its advantages.

Before Mike Adcock and I would give anyone their steak, we would tear out the best part of it and eat it. If anyone complained, well, that's just too bad.

After we had been thoroughly humiliated, we were allowed to sit down and eat, too. But I wasn't very hungry—I was too full to eat.

April 20

Big news for the seniors today. The coaches say they will hold Pro Day on Monday. Pro Day is a day when scouts from the National Football League (and, I guess, the United States Football League, too) come in and test potential players.

The scouts put you through a variety of written tests and evaluate your running and jumping ability. If you do well, you may even be drafted next year.

I can take the pros or leave them, but Larry Brown wants to make the pros in the worse way. Larry, who was a tight end last year but a graduate assistant coach this spring, asked me to help him with his "starts."

A coach asking *me* for help? I was flattered.

I was visiting Mike Adcock and Randy Edward tonight when I noticed that Randy was unusually grumpy.

"What's wrong with Randy?" I asked Mike.

"Ah," Mike said, "he's just mad because I beat him in one-on-one drills today."

It's pride I tell you. Next time out, Randy will beat Mike or die trying.

April 21

Major milestone today.

Had another scrimmage and paid the defense back for all the misery they have caused us. We moved the ball well and scored every time we had it. Our confidence is at an all-time high.

We put in some new option plays which had the defense thoroughly confused. The option is really ticking for us. I think that's because we were used to option plays from the old wishbone.

It felt great being on the winning side for a change.

Wes Neighbors is either one of the bravest players on this team or one of the craziest. I haven't figured out which.

While Jon Hand was attending a meeting after practice, Wes got Jon's helmet out of the locker and began wrapping it in adhesive tape. He must have used three rolls of tape because by the time he was finished, Jon's helmet was one big ball of tape. You couldn't see any of the helmet for all the tape on it.

When Big Jon returned from the meeting, his taped-up helmet was in his locker waiting for him. Wes sat a safe distance away, neatly folding his clothes—the picture of childlike innocence. Everyone else quietly watched out of the corner of their eyes as Jon pulled the helmet from his locker.

"Ha, ha," big Jon said. "Oh, this *is* funny. Ha. Ha. Now, that I've laughed, I don't suppose that whoever did this is going to show their face, are they?"

Dead silence.

"No, I thought not."

Big Jon is 6-foot-7 and weighs 280. Would *you* have told him?

No, I thought not.

April 24

My expert advice has helped Larry Brown cut two-tenths of a second off of his 40-yard dash time, and with Pro Day coming up tomorrow, he was ever so thankful.

A couple of scouts told me last week that they had been watching some film on me, but I don't know if that means anything.

One scout asked me how big I was. I told him 5-9, 167, but I felt like saying, "Big enough!"

Oh well, maybe Larry Brown will recommend me for a coaching job. . .

April 25

Everything was working against me, but I believe I came out of Pro Day all right.

The day started badly because my knee was bothering me. And when speed is the best thing you have going for you, you can't afford to be slowed down by a bum knee.

So, I went to the equipment room and asked Willie Meadows for a pair of "grass shoes."

"What do you need grass shoes for?!" Willie demanded.

"Because the pro scouts are going to be timing us in the 40, and I can't run in artificial turf shoes—there's no grip," I explained.

"You don't need any grass shoes," he argued. "Get outta here!"

"OK!" I said angrily, "But you're probably costing me my whole career!"

I stormed out of the equipment room and headed to the practice field where the scouts were waiting. I ran through a few warmups to loosen up and my knee was still hurting. I was convinced this just wasn't my day.

Sure enough, on my first 40-yard dash I stumbled on the start. I did manage to recover near the end. When I returned to the starting line, I asked the scouts how I did.

"Four-point-four seconds," one scout said. "That's not bad."

"I can do better," I said.

"Good!" he said. "We're going to time you again so get back in line."

I got back in line and waited my turn again, all the time secretly praying that my knee would stop hurting. It did. And the next time out, I ran a 4.3.

"That's the fastest time I've seen on natural grass in 16 years!" exclaimed a scout for the Los Angeles Raiders.

"Oh, really?" I said, trying to remain humble.

"Yeah, really," he said. "Do you usually run that fast?"

"Well," I said. "I *have* run a 4.2 before."

After that, everything went much better. I did well on my pass catching, on the vertical jumps and the half-dozen other things they had us do. I may even have passed that written exam.

So like I said before, I think I did all right. But I'm not about to go out and buy a new Jaguar XKE.

I wanted to ask Coach Perkins if it would be OK if I went to summer school this semester, so I had to go see him in his office.

It was a scary feeling, a lot like the one I'd get when I went to see Coach Bryant. When I walked in, his office door was closed. I asked Coach Perkins' secretary, Marilyn Rowell, if it was all right if I went in.

"Sure," she said, "Go ahead and knock."

So I took a deep breath and raised my hand. Then, I stopped.

"Go ahead!" Marilyn said. "Knock! He won't mind."

So I took another deep breath, summoned up all my courage and knocked.

"Come on in," came the reply from behind the door.

I nervously entered the room, stood before his desk and popped the question.

"Coach, is it all right if I stay up here for summer school?"

I was expecting a "Why sure, Joey! Glad to see you studying

this way!" Or something like that. Instead, he glared at me and his lips turned into that half-smile, half-sneer of his.

"Why!" he said. It was an order, not a question.

"Well, uh," I stuttered, "'Cause I want to graduate next spring and I can if I go all summer."

"I don't want you up here for football purposes. I don't want you up here working on football."

"Well," I said, "It's not that. I really need to do it so I can graduate."

"That's fine," he said. "If you need to do it to graduate, that's fine. I hope you graduate on time, but I don't want you up here working on football all summer. You need a break. You need to get home and see your family."

You have to respect a guy for that.

April 26

After practice today everyone was talking about what they planned to do this summer when Randy Edwards noticed that Paul Carruth was still healthy.

"Hey, Paul!" he shouted across the room, "You've made it through 19 practices now. You're not going to disappoint us, are you?"

I think Randy's just jealous. He's been limping around on a pulled hamstring most the spring.

Maybe I did better than I thought in Pro Day.

I was in the weight room, working on the bench press, when Coach Miller walked in and said, "Joey Jones, come over here."

I put down the weights and walked over to Coach Miller.

"Joey," he said, "I just talked to a scout for the San Diego Chargers yesterday, and he said that if you get your butt in this weight room, work hard, gain about 10 pounds and maintain your speed, you're going to be up for a lot of money next year."

"No kidding?" I asked incredulously.

"That's right," he said. "Are you going to be up here this summer?"

"Yes, sir."

"Good, because I'm going to have you faster than a jackrabbit and harder than a sack of hammers."

How can I ever thank him?

April 27

Well, Paul almost made it.

We got down to the very last play of our very last scrimmage when Steve Booker burst through the line and nailed Paul on a sweep around right end. Paul lay crumpled on the ground, his hands covering his eyes because he was afraid to look at his right knee. It scared the heck out of me and made Booker feel terrible.

As Coach Goostree helped him off the field, I ran up and asked Paul how he was doing.

"He's all right!" Coach Goostree snapped. "You just leave him alone."

"Look!" I said, getting angry, "I'm just trying to find out how my rommate is doing! Paul, are you all right?"

"It hurts," Paul said, gritting his teeth as he limped along, "but I'll be OK."

"All right," I said. "I'll see you back at the dorm."

It was a very bad way to end the spring.

April 28

I was expecting last night's spring awards banquet to be just another banquet where you sat and were bored to tears. I was wrong.

We had all the catfish we could eat, some players put on some funny skits, and then came the awards. Freddie Robinson won the "Bobby Johns Most Improved Defensive Back" award, Jon Hand won the "Billy Neighbors Most Improved Defensive Lineman" award, George Salem won the "Jerry Duncan I Like to Practice" award, and Wes Neighbors won the "Paul Crane Most Improved Offensive Lineman" award.

Then, in an upset, I won the "Ray Perkins Most Improved Receiver" award. When I went up to accept the award and shake Coach Perkins' hand, I'll never forget the way he looked at me. You could tell that the award meant a lot to him.

Paul Carruth won the "Johnny Musso Most Improved Offensive Back" award, but I had to accept the award for him because Paul was still laid up in our room with his knee all bandaged up.

When I returned to the dorm last night, I had Paul's award behind my back. I popped through the door, waving my award in

Paul's face.

"Look, Paul," I said, "I got one!"

"Great!" he said. "I'm proud of you."

"Yeah," I said, bringing his award from behind my back, "and it looks like my roomie gets one, too."

"Aww-right!" he said.

You should have seen his face light up.

Coach Goostree hasn't yet figured out exactly what is wrong with Paul's knee. The knee isn't swelling, and that's usually a bad sign. I'm afraid there may be cartilage damage.

April 30

Championship talk is beginning. I've heard it before, but this time, I believe it's for real.

Randy Edwards, Paul Carruth, Mike Adcock and I were sitting around last night, talking about our chances of winning the national championship this fall. We believe we can do it.

In the past when somebody talked championship around here, we all more or less sat back expecting it to come to us on a silver platter simply because we were Alabama.

But we're tired of walking off the field a loser now. It's not going to happen unless we make it happen. We've got to stop living in the past. We're a new Alabama team now, and we've got to start our own winning tradition.

Footnote: Paul's knee is feeling worse. He says a specialist is coming in Monday to look at it.

May 2

Saw Paul in the room packing, and I asked him where he was going.

"New York," he said.

"New York? Why New York?" I asked. "That specialist says I've got a torn cartilage and I need surgery right away. Coach

Perkins wants me to go to New York to let the Giants' team doctor do the surgery."

May 3

Took my last exam today, and then went to see Coach Miller, who gave me a running and weight program to work on while I'm away.

I also had a one-on-one interview with Coach Felker about my goals for this fall.

"My goal for this fall," I told him, "is to win the national championship. And I want us to be able to get there by being able to count on me on third-and-long situations. I want Walter to be able to call for that 15-yard 'in' route with confidence that I can catch it."

Coach Felker was impressed.

Well, I've got my clothes packed in a clothes basket, and I'm ready to head home to Mobile for a month of relaxation.

Look out, Gulf Shores, here I come!

PART VII

Gimme a Break!

May 14
Gulf Shores

Well, here I am—laid back in Lower Alabama, lying on the white sands of the Redneck Riviera, and sipping suds at the L. A. Pub 'n Grub.

What a life!

I love it here. I love lying on the beach, smelling the surf and the aroma of coconut suntan oil hanging in the thick summer air. I love listening to the waves beating against the rocks. And I love watching the girls.

Everybody needs a break sometime and I spend my leisure hours on the beach. I'm convinced that a good, dark tan has psychological advantages. If you report back in the fall with a good tan, the coaches think you're in shape. If you come back pale looking, they think you've spent the entire summer indoors under the air conditioner. And if Coach Miller thinks you're out of shape, he will put you on an accelerated weight program that can darn near kill you. So, in my thinking, a little "red" is better than "dead."

Still, it's hard to get away from football on this tropical paradise made famous by Ken Stabler. Even without that No. 4 jersey hanging on my back, I often find myself cornered by fans wanting to know what's in store for Alabama football this fall.

Just yesterday, I was standing at a bar with two friends, Mike Davenport and Stanley Morrow, when some elderly man walked up from behind and slapped me on the back.

"Aren't you Joey Jones?" the man asked.

"Err. . .yes, sir," I said, turning around.

"Reckon ol' Ray can fill the Bear's shoes, Joey?" he went on.

"Yes, sir," I said, "I believe so."

Mike and Stanley immediately sensed I was headed for an hour-long discussion on Alabama football, and bailed me out.

"Joey, let's go play some video games." Mike said.

"Yeah, come on," Stanley agreed, grabbing my arm.

I could have kissed them both.

May 16
Mobile

Called Paul Carruth in New York today to see how my roomie was doing. The report wasn't good. He says he is bored to death lying in the hospital, and his knee is still hurting.

"I keep yelling for the nurse to bring pain pills," Paul said, "but she only brings one at a time. I told her I needed enough for two weeks."

He also said that Coach Perkins' wife, Carolyn, has been spending almost every day with him.

The surgery apparently went OK, but Paul did not say whether he could play this fall. I was afraid to ask.

May 30

My roomie has returned home to Mississippi, but he's feeling awfully low.

"Coach Perkins and Coach Goostree said it would be best to sit this season out rather than going through a whole season injured and trying to rehabilitate it from week to week," Paul said. "I know they're right, but I sure was counting on playing."

June 5
Tuscaloosa

I received a welcome home bigger than life today. Driving into town on 15th Street, I was greeted by a huge billboard that read, "Catch the Excitement of Alabama Football." On it were life-size sketches of Jesse Bendross, Coach Perkins, and myself, all drawn by Jimmy Tom Goostree.

And I remember when I got excited seeing my name in the *Mobile Press Register*. . .

Home is where my clothes are. And right now, my clothes are piled in a laundry basket in the corner of a rather small room at Friedman Hall.

Arriving at Bryant Hall, I encountered dozens of high school kids walking around the campus and wearing Pony painter's caps and red T-shirts.

"Where did all these kids come from?" I asked Coach Rutledge as I went in to register at Bryant Hall.

"They're here for Coach Perkins' football camp," he said. "They'll be here for about a week, and we're going to have to put the team over at Friedman Hall for awhile."

"You mean they're staying here in the dorm?"

"Yep. That's where Coach Perkins wants them. There's nothing I can do."

"Well, dern it! Where's Friedman Hall? Is it a dump?"

"No, it's not so bad," he said. "It's the old athletic dormitory. Besides, it's just for a few days."

But Coach Rutledge was wrong—Friedman *is* a dump. The plumbing is bad, the place smells like a broken urinal, and the air conditioning makes an awful racket.

June 6

My room here at Friedman Hall is becoming more crowded all the time. Paul came back late yesterday afternoon, wearing his knee brace, and moved in. And then Mike White and Kurt Schmissrauter also moved in. So we now have four people living in one cramped space.

Make that five—Mike Adcock just joined us.

Mike burst through the door 10 minutes ago, dragging a mattress behind him.

"They've got me sharing a room with a guy who wears hair curlers!" he roared as he threw the mattress down in the middle of our floor. "I know you are crowded, but I'm moving in."

I guess I can stand it for a few days.

June 7

Paul tells me that the reason all these high school kids are wearing Pony caps is because Coach Perkins has signed a contract with the Pony Shoe Company.

"Looks like you'll be wearing Pony shoes this season," Paul said. "You'll probably have to," Paul said. "Everybody will have to."

"Not me," I said firmly. "I'll keep my old Nikes and paint a Pony stripe on them."

June 10

Another Alabama legend has been swept out the door. John Forney, the radio voice of the Alabama Football Network for the past 19 years, has been replaced. Paul Kennedy, a former Vanderbilt promotions man who Coach Perkins hired several days ago, will now handle the play-by-play.

This has not been a popular move around here. Many fans grew up listening to Forney's voice on Saturday afternoons and had become accustomed to his voice. A student in my finance class is so mad about it that he said, "I hope Ray Perkins falls flat on his face."

I really can't understand this attraction to radio announcers. To me, the only thing that counts is the final score—not who tells you about it. Maybe I'm missing the point, but then, I never listen to games on the radio anyway.

June 15

I'm going to have to read the papers more often.

I just finished reading a story in the *Birmingham News* about all the personnel changes Coach Perkins has made over the past few weeks. I didn't realize there were so many.

I didn't know that Coach Clem Gryska, our recruiting coordinator, has gone into semi-retirement. Nor did I realize that Jack Perry, the head of the sports information department, had resigned and been replaced by Wayne Atcheson. And I was sorry to read that Coach Perkins has hired Mike Hogewood from WBRC-TV in Birmingham to co-host his television show. Hogewood's on-the-air delivery is so bubbly that he always seems to be on the verge of laughter.

Paul Carruth now tells me that there will not only be one Ray Perkins TV show this fall, but *two*. One will be aired on Thursday nights, the other on Sunday afternoons. And, Paul says, Perkins will have a radio call-in show similar to Coach Bryant's "Bearline," as well as daily progress reports on the radio each morning.

Maybe I'm from the old school, but I don't like all this promotion business. Too much is too much. After all, it's not like we're having trouble selling tickets to Alabama football games. . .

June 21

Did I mention that summer school is a bore? It is.

Every night brings another reading assignment, and every week brings another exam. A fellow can't get a moment's peace.

Luckily, I met a girl in my class, Kristy Jarrell, who had access to some old tests through one of the sorority houses. That may just pull me through this finance course.

Just heard on the radio that the City of Tuscaloosa plans to rename Tenth Street "Paul W. Bryant Drive." This is the street that runs from I-359, past Memorial Drive and Druid City Hospital.

The city traffic engineer says that extra measures will be taken to make certain the street signs are securely fastened to avert potential souvenir hunters.

Sounds like an invitation to me. . .

June 29

Just heard that Chuckie Fields has left the team to spend more time studying. Usually that is the excuse the sports information office uses to hide a deep, dark secret, but that's not the case with Chuckie. He says he just felt like he wouldn't get much of an opportunity to play, and that his time would be better spent studying. He wants to become a coach, and I have no doubt that he will be a good one.

July 1

Plenty of rumors flying around about new uniforms.

Paul Carruth says that we'll be wearing white helmets at times this fall so that Walter Lewis can find the receivers more easily in a crowd.

"White helmets?" I asked.

"Yeah," said Paul, "but only when the other team is wearing a dark-colored helmet."

"Didn't they wear white helmets when Coach Perkins played here?" I asked.

"Yes. . .why?"

"Oh, no reason. It just seems like he's trying to change things back to the way they were when he played here."

But the helmets aren't the only change. Paul also says that the jerseys won't have our names on back this year, but will have bigger numbers instead.

Kurt Schmissrauter should like that. They always had to abbreviate his name anyway.

July 2

Just when I thought Coach Perkins was trying to erase all memory of Coach Bryant, he comes up with a way of honoring him. He says we will be wearing decals of a houndstooth hat on the back of our helmets this fall. I like that idea.

July 8

Nearly every poll I have seen has picked Auburn to win the Southeastern Conference championship this season.

So, when *Tuscaloosa News* sports editor Billy Mitchell asked Coach Perkins about that, Coach Perkins replied this way in Mitchell's column today: "Winning the conference championship is not our goal and it's never been the goal around here. Winning the national championship has always been the goal at Alabama and it's no different this year."

Hoo-ey! Take that, Auburn!

July 10
Bryant Hall

Home, sweet, home.

After a month of being cramped in Friedman Hall, Paul and I are finally back home in our spacious third-floor room at Bryant Hall. I feel as if I've escaped from a sardine can. I'll never say a bad thing about Bryant Hall again.

Alabama football has gone co-ed. Several days ago Coach Perkins hired Sydnie Kohara from WSFA-TV in Montgomery to co-host the Thursday night TV show. I'm going to refrain from all chauvinistic remarks about women and football, and simply say, "Welcome aboard, Sydnie."

July 12

And on the Twelfth Day, the Lord said, "Let there be freshmen." And there were—dozens of them.

Never before have I seen so many freshmen roaming around the dormitory in July. What are they doing here so early? They don't have to report until August 13!

Bill Jordan, a freshman lineman from Geneva, must have arrived in a tractor trailer truck. He's 6-foot-7 and weighs at least 300 pounds. Other freshmen I've seen today include: Craig Epps, a linebacker from Miami; big Curt Jarvis, a lineman from Gardendale; Alan Brown, another big lineman from Ken Coley's old school in Birmingham; Larry Abney, a quarterback from Slidell, Louisiana; Tim Hecht, a quarterback from Vienna, Virginia; Ricky Thomas, a defensive back from Niceville, Florida; Wayne Davis, a linebacker from Gordo; Hugh Smith, a walk-on quarterback from Linnie Patrick's old school in Jasper; and Mike Shula.

Freshmen don't talk very much, which is good because freshmen have no rights at all. I remember when I was a freshman you were treated like the scum of the earth. In team meetings, you were more or less pushed aside and forgotten. If there was a line to be formed, the freshman stood at the end of it. When there was a meal served, the freshmen were the last to eat.

It can be a pretty traumatic experience. We call it the

"freshmen blues.' Everybody gets it at one time or another. And when you do, you're ready to walk out. I remember seeing Dante Bramblett pack his bags one night and vow to go home. I even thought about packing mine before. But you get over it. You stop running up $200 phone bills and you stop running home to mamma everytime something doesn't go your way.

Before you know it, you've grown into somebody special—a senior.

July 13

Coach Miller has created a monster and named it Randy Edwards.

When spring practice ended, Randy looked like the Pillsbury Dough Boy—round and smooth. Now, Randy looks like the Incredible Hulk with muscle stacked upon muscle.

"Have you been taking steroids?" I asked him.

"You know I wouldn't take those," he said. "What you see is all me."

"Well, you must've been doing something," I said. "You've blown up like a helium balloon."

What Randy has been doing is working hard. He got himself an apartment along with John McIntosh and Rob Roberts, and they've spent the whole summer up here painting Bryant-Denny Stadium. After painting all day, Randy heads straight for the weight room.

But I don't want to give you the impression that Randy is the only one who has been working hard. In fact, there are at least 70 players on campus now, and Coach Miller is putting us all through a rigorous exercise program. He has even brought in an extra coach to train us in Olympic weight lifting. It's really paid off. This team is in better shape than any team since I've been here. Jesse Bendross has lost 25 pounds during the summer and picked up some extra speed, and Linnie Patrick is working harder than I've ever seen him work. My only regret is that Jon Hand isn't here. If Coach Miller had been working with him, a Mack truck couldn't stop Jon Hand this fall.

John McIntosh tells me that he and Rob Roberts caught

Randy Edwards sleeping in the portals at the stadium yesterday when he was supposed to be working. So while Randy slept, they painted his shoes red and white.

July 22

Rodney Jarmon became an academic casualty today and will be out for the entire season. This is a terrible loss for our defensive secondary. One of the younger players suggested the coaches help Rodney out by "doctoring" his grades.

"You know they're not going to do that," I said. "They think we came here for an education!"

The pen is mightier than the sword. Rodney will just have to dig in with his books, take a few "Wood Bending" courses, and give it another shot next season.

July 31

Headlines across the top of the *Tuscaloosa News* sports pages today read, "Bama recruits have Perkins enthused."

To which Randy Edwards replied, "When we were freshmen, they never talked that way about us. The only time you'd ever see a freshman's name even mentioned was usually just a short paragraph listing their name and hometown."

Good point, Randy.

August 3

The new media guides are out and Yours Truly appears on Pages 3, 24, 25, 87, and 89. I know because I looked. The media guides are intended for sports writers who cover our games, but every player looks on these as a yearbook of sorts. And we love to read what it says in there about us.

My biographical sketch starts off like this: "There are two major reasons head coach Ray Perkins has gone to the pro-set offense—Joey Jones and Jesse Bendross. The pair gives the Crimson Tide the best one-two punch at receiver since Dennis Homan and Perkins himself combined for the Tide in the 1960s. . ." Pretty heady stuff, huh? Wait—there's more. My statistics for last season read: Games played, 11; receptions, 25;

yards, 502; average, 20.0; touchdowns, 8; and long reception, 38. That brings my career statistics to 32 games played, 40 receptions for 918 yards, an average of 23 yards per catch, 10 touchdowns, and a long reception of 81 yards. I don't want to brag, kiddies, but that ain't bad for the wishbone.

But insecure as I am, I just had to check Jesse Bendross' biography—just to make sure, you know. His reads, "In a revamped offense that is geared to the pass, Jesse may be the happiest person on the Crimson Tide football team. After leading the team in receptions two years ago, Jesse came back last year and tied fellow receiver Joey Jones with 25..." Fair enough. Now for Jesse's stats: games played, 11; receptions, 25; yards, 499; average, 19.9; touchdowns, 8; and long reception, 80.

I was glowing with satisfaction with this fair treatment when Paul Carruth screamed out, "What?! I'm not even in here!" Sure enough, Paul has been omitted from this year's media guide, except for a cameo appearance in an action shot on Page 74.

"I can't believe that!" Paul exclaimed. "I practice every day in the spring, and they don't even put me in there because I got hurt! That's ridiculous! Boy, I can see now that they aren't counting on me in all this year."

"Aw, that's not so bad, Paul," I said, trying to cheer him up. "Look at it this way—they could have put you in there and you'd come out looking like Randy Edwards looks in his picture—like Frankenstein!"

August 7

Prescribed reading in today's *Tuscaloosa News* is Billy Mitchell's column on Coach Rutledge.

The story is about how Coach Rutledge came to be the dorm director and how he keeps 132 athletes in order. In one interesting anecdote, he tells about separating two roommates who had gotten into a fight. He wouldn't say who they were, but if my memory serves me correctly, I remember the time he kept Linnie Patrick and Jerry Lambert from killing one another. It was my freshman year and Jerry and Linnie were roomies. They had been playfully wrestling around when things got out of hand. Jerry would charge Linnie like a mad bull, but Linnie would just pick him up and throw him 10 feet across the hall. Linnie tried getting

Jerry to stop, but Jerry kept coming. "Man, I'm gonna have to hurt you," Linnie would say. But Jerry kept coming and Linnie kept throwing him. Finally, Coach Rutledge came in and broke it up. The show was over.

August 12

Flash from Hollywood: Gary Busey has been chosen to portray Coach Bryant in the movie "Bear." All I want to know is, "Who's Gary Busey?"

Didn't I say Greg Richardson was fast? In freshman physicals today, he ran the 40-yard dash in 4.38. That matches the speed I ran for the NFL scouts on Pro Day. Looks like my reputation as the team's fastest player may be in danger.

August 15

The freshmen are into two-a-day practices now, and our time will be coming up in just a few days. But in the meantime, we love teasing the freshmen about having to work out in this hot weather while we go swimming.

But actually, these freshmen have it easy compared to my freshman year. These freshmen don't start practice until 9 a.m., while we had to get up at 5:30 to make Coach Bryant's 7 a.m. practices. I'm telling you, they have it easy.

As always, though, many freshmen are discovering that the position they played in high school is not necessarily the position you will play in college. Larry Abney found himself at cornerback as practice began, Curt Jarvis has been moved to nose guard, Dante Knox is now at free safety, and Cornelius Bennett is now at outside linebacker.

August 16

Back to the salt mines. The varsity reported for physicals today. The only running I had been doing was sprints so I did poorly in the mile run—5 minutes, 40 seconds. And since I ran it in 5:12 last fall, I took a lot of harassment.

"You just cruised it didn't you?" Coach Felker said as I plopped down in the grass.

"Yep," I said, gasping for air.

"Didn't want to strain yourself did you?" he asked with a gleam in his eye.

"No," I replied. "I'm just saving myself for tomorrow, Coach."

Unfortunately, people like Jesse Bendross had to show me up by running it in 5:01. Fortunately, there was still Linnie Patrick, who ran it in about 6:30.

For some reason, the mile run has always fascinated the hardcore fans. They seem to think that your time is an indication of what kind of season is in store for you. But that's not always the case.

Then again, sometimes it is the case. I remember one fall when Jeff Bohannon, a big lineman, was huffing and puffing his way around the track. Everyone else had finished their mile run, but Bohannon still had two laps to go and was about to drop.

Suddenly, Coach Bryant began yelling at the assistant coaches: "Get him off the track! Get him off the track right now before he dies!"

Jeff Bohannon never played football at Alabama.

Our new curfew is now in effect—11:30 as opposed to the old midnight curfew. This, of course, created the usual bickering.

"What difference does 30 minutes make?" David Valletto asked. "We can come in at 11:30 just as easily as we can at 12!"

Which reminds me of the joke about the girl who said, "If I'm not in bed by 11:30, I'm going home."

August 17

The last thing a player wants to do when there is no afternoon practice is to put on a full uniform and stand in the hot sun for two hours while photographers take your picture. But that's Picture Day. And everybody hates it.

Everybody, that is, except my poor roomie, Paul Carruth. Paul is feeling left out these days. He stood around with his knee brace on, and nobody called on him for a picture or an interview.

To make things worse, Ernest Carroll, a walk-on quarterback from West Blocton, was wearing Paul's jersey number.

"A walk-on?" Paul said. "What an insult!"

The mystery question of the week is: "Where's Perry Cuda?"

August 18

Found a pair of Pony shoes in my locker before practice today. I carried them back to Willie Meadows and told him, "Thanks, but no thanks. I'll keep my Nikes."

But Willie was insistent.

"You may as well get used to them," he said. "Coach Perkins has signed a contract with Pony, and you'll have to wear them in the games."

I could see there was no use in fighting it. I took the shoes outside, beat them into the dirt and rubbed some grass stains on them. I hate new shoes—especially new white ones.

The rumor mill has it that Perry Cuda has gone home and is considering tranferring to another school. I hope this isn't so. We need Perry—if not this year, then definitely next season.

August 20

Every time I forget how dangerous football can be something happens to remind me of it again.

I thought about that this afternoon when I heard that Greg Pratt, a fullback at Auburn, had collapsed and died after running four 440-meter sprints. Like me, he was 20 years old.

I love football, but it can be dangerous. When you walk onto that field, there is always the chance you won't walk off it. Rules, safer equipment and extensive conditioning programs have reduced the risk but not eliminated them. Still, we continue to put our bodies (and yes, even lives) on the line just for the sake of a game.

We put on the pads today, but we didn't get much accomplished. The SEC Sky Writers tour came through, and much of the afternoon practice was taken up with newspaper and television interviews. I was just beginning to enjoy all this media attention when a thunderstorm came and chased the Sky Writers away. So, we moved into Memorial Coliseum and walked through a few plays.

Oh yes, still no sign of Perry Cuda.

I think I'm finally getting my head on right about Coach Perkins. I really like the man—really. He's sincere, dedicated, enthusiastic, and everything else that Boy Scouts strive to be.

Tonight's meeting was very casual and laid-back. I guess Coach Perkins was feeling more relaxed than usual because he seemed looser, more at ease with us than he has shown before. He apologized for waiting so long to talk to us about the endless comparisons that are made between himself and Coach Bryant.

"I've talked to everybody else that has asked me about it," he said, "But I haven't talked to the most important people—you.

"Coach Bryant was the greatest man and greatest coach who ever lived. I respected him and I loved him. There will never be another man like him. I can't be like him. I don't intend to be. The only way I can follow a man like him is by being myself. . ."

OK, so it isn't anything we haven't already read in the newspapers. But at least it's a start.

After awhile, he dismissed everyone but the seniors. He became even more at ease and began reminiscing about the fun he used to have in the old "A Club" and "Letterman's Club." He made it sound so good that we asked him if we could start the clubs up again.

"Sure," he said. "I'm all for it. We'll get the Letterman's Club back for sure, and we'll try to get the A Club back. You just have to be careful about the initiations.

"What I'm going to say you can do is this—you can have the initiation, but just don't do anything that will harm the players. Judge it for yourself. Do whatever you want, but just don't harm the players.

"We'll have to keep it quiet. There has been so much trouble with people getting killed and hurt in fraternity initiations that they've had to ban them. They'll be watching you—we're really not supposed to do it. So if you do it, I don't want to know anything about it. Just don't harm the players."

August 23

Joe Carter gave us a scare today.

Joe was showering after another extremely hot practice when he suddenly grabbed the calf of his left leg as if he had been stung by a bee. Then he grabbed his left shoulder with the other hand. Within seconds, Joe was lying contorted on the floor, twitching and shaking all over. Even his fingers on both hands were curled up like claws.

Someone ran and got Coach Goostree, who helped Joe into the training room and placed him on a training table. They packed him in ice and inserted I.V. tubes into his arm.

"Heat stroke," I said to myself, and immediately thought about Greg Pratt.

Fortunately, my diagnosis was wrong. It was only muscle cramps.

Since Greg Pratt died, the coaches have been very careful with us. We're having more water breaks than ever, and there's always a large supply of ice on the field. Still, it's too hot for football.

August 24

Perry Cuda has quit the team. Why, I don't know.

"I've talked with Perry and he has decided he doesn't want to play," Coach Perkins said in a team meeting. "Now reporters are going to be coming around asking questions. They are going to try to get you to say something bad about him, but I don't want to hear any bad remarks about him. Perry did what he thought was right, and we've got to back him up."

And that was that.

August 27

And now, ladies and gentlemen, for a day in the life of a certain split end. . .

My daily routine:

        6:00 a.m.—Wake up.
        7-7:30 a.m.—Eat breakfast.
        7:30-8:30 a.m.—Receivers meeting.
        8:30-9 a.m.—Dress for practice.
        9-11:30 a.m.—Practice.
        11:30-12:30 p.m.—Eat lunch.
        12:30-1 p.m.—Watch "All My Children"
        1-3 p.m.—More meetings.
        3-5 p.m—Catch your breath.
        5-7:30 p.m.—Practice.
        7:30-8 p.m.—Eat dinner.
        8:15-10:30 p.m.—Still more meetings.
        10:30-11:30 p.m.—Shower and shave.
        11:30 p.m.—Lights out.

Well, gotta run. . .it's time for a scrimmage.

August 28

Ah, Sunday. Two-a-day practices are over at last. I slept until 11:30 this morning and enjoyed every minute of it. Everybody likes to sleep late on Sundays, especially after two-a-days have ended.

But Dante Bramblett reminds me of the time when we received a rude awakening on a peaceful Sunday morning. It was late August of our sophomore year when Coach Bryant made a rare appearance at Bryant Hall. He had planned to have breakfast with the team, but discovered the cafeteria was deserted. Being told that everyone was still sleeping, he began going from room to room, knocking on the door and telling each occupant to get his fanny to breakfast.

When he reached Robbie Jones' room and began pounding away on the door, unsuspecting Robbie told him to get lost.

"What the hell do you want at this hour?" Robbie yelled. "Who is it!"

No answer.

Knock. Knock. Knock.

Angered by this persistent knocking, Robbie jumped out of

bed and threw the door open.

"Oh! Er uh, good morning, Coach."

"You better get your ass out of bed and down to breakfast, son!"

"Yes, sir! Yes, sir!"

Word spread quickly that Coach Bryant was making the rounds. By the time Coach Bryant returned to the cafeteria, the breakfast line was a mile long.

Arriving at practice yesterday, I found a new jersey in my locker—jersey number 80.

"What's this?" I wondered. Then I looked around the room and saw that everyone had different jersey numbers.

"Uh, oh," I thought, "Coach Perkins smells a rat."

It's not unusual for football coaches to become paranoid at this time of year. They fear someone may be spying on us in an attempt to pick up on a few team secrets or player tendencies. When this happens, coaches take extra precautions such as assigning different jersey numbers for players during scrimmages or closing off practice to all unfamiliar faces.

I can only asusme that this new wave of paranoia was ushered in by the recent Tulane spy caper. Gerald Materne, a Tulane graduate assistant, made headlines last week when he was caught red-handed while hiding in the bushes at a Mississippi State practice. Embarrassed, Tulane officials disavowed any knowledge of Materne's actions.

So yesterday scrimmage was closed. A few members of the press were allowed in only after consenting to not report on individual performances. Our managers parked a pickup truck near a gap in the fence and made occasional rounds to make certain nobody was hidden in the bushes.

We were safe from everything but spy satellites.

PART VIII

Let the Games Begin

August 29
Bryant Hall

Power of positive thinking tells me that the Crimson Tide is going to roll this year.

Surprised?

I am.

When Coach Bryant retired and Coach Perkins took over, I thought there would be no way we could be a good team this season. Everything seemed so uncertain, so strange. But now that I look over our schedule, assess our strengths and weaknesses, I think it's very possible to win all 11 games.

Of course, the first four games *should* be a breeze. Georgia Tech, Ole Miss, Vanderbilt and Memphis State aren't exactly football powerhouses. And yet, there is no such thing as an "automatic win."

Naturally, we will be heavily favored in these four games. But after that, it doesn't get any easier. Our first real test comes October 8 when we play Penn State at State College, Pennsylvania. Penn State is traditionally a tough team, and it will have the advantage of having an extra game under its belt by the time we play them. They kick off the season tonight against Nebraska in the first Kickoff Classic.

Tennessee comes to Birmingham on October 15. That's always a tough game because of the rivalry between us. After Tennessee, we'll take a weekend off before playing Mississippi State in Tuscaloosa. State is another one of those teams we usually beat, but have a hard time doing so. It's always a low-scoring, defensive game.

We travel to Baton Rouge on November 5 to play LSU in Tiger Stadium. Since they humiliated us last season, I'm looking forward to playing them again.

The best trip of the year is to Foxboro, Massachusetts on November 25 to play Boston College. BC, as they are commonly called, is supposed to be great this year. Their quarterback, Doug Flutie, is being touted as a Heisman Trophy candidate. But with a week off to prepare for them, we should be all right there.

The bad part of having an off week before the BC game is that we won't have our traditional open date before the Auburn game on December 3. This is strictly poor planning on somebody's part. As much as I hate to admit it, Auburn is going to be tough to be beat this year. They have more returning starters than any team in the SEC and are sound through and through. But, like I said before, I like our chances.

Another reason I like our chances of a successful season is because of the harmony on this team. I'm talking about the way all the players get along with one another. We enjoy our time together, both on and off the field. I guess we have Coach Perkins to thank for that. When he came in and started making all these changes it drew us closer together. It was us against them. Since then, the alienation between coaches and players has virtually disappeared. We realize we're all in the same boat.

Oddly enough, it's Linnie Patrick—the one player the press enjoys portraying as a malcontent—who keeps us loose.

It was Linnie who gave Wes Neighbors the nickname "Round Head" because his head is shaped like a bowling ball. And it was Linnie who first began calling Desmond Holomon "Gadzuki" after the cartoon nephew of Godzilla.

Other nicknames have been around for quite awhile. Paul Fields has been "Pablo" since Coach Bryant nicknamed him that three years ago, and Tom McCrary has been "Chewy" or "Chewbacca" (after the *Star Wars* character) for almost as long. Anthony Smiley has been "Pips" since the day I pinched the thick muscle on the back of his neck, and he replied, "hey, man, don't go messing with my pip."

Mike Shula is "Shoe Box."

Walter Lewis is "Tank Head."

Kurt Schmissrauter is "Michelin Man."

And Billy Pierce is "Otis."

Why, Otis, you ask?

Did you ever see "The Andy Griffith Show?"

So, you can see, we're one big happy family.

A note on the bulletin board in the cafeteria reads, "Team Meeting, 7:30 p.m., Tonight, Annex."

Don't let that fool you. If two-a-days have just ended, this means only one thing—it's freshman initiation time!

August 30

The Grinch has stolen Christmas.

Well, it really wasn't the Grinch—it was Coach Jack Rutledge. And it really wasn't Christmas, of course, but it was the next best thing—freshmen initiation.

Everything was all set last night. The freshmen were up in their rooms, getting out of their clothes and into their jock straps. The tribunal of seniors were dressed in their finest initiation togas and waiting in the dormitory annex; and the rest of us were scurrying around, putting the finishing touches on a wide variety of foul-smelling concoctions which we planned to make the freshmen drink.

Then in came The Governor and stopped the show.

"What are you guys up to?" he asked, as if he didn't know.

"Freshman initiation!" came the rousing reply.

"Not this year," he said. "There aren't supposed to be any initiations any more. You guys know that. It's against the rules."

"But Coach Perkins said it was OK as long as we didn't do anything to hurt the players," protested Randy Edwards. "He said it was all right."

"I don't know anything about that," Coach Rutledge said. "All I know is that I want this mess cleaned up and you guys out of here in 15 minutes."

With that, The Governor turned and walked out. It was probably a good thing that he did, too. Otherwise, it might have become a really nasty scene.

It was all we could do to keep Randy Edwards under control. Randy has been waiting for this day for four long years.

Now that he was a senior, he wanted to do the initiating. He had even gone to the trouble of dressing for the occasion—a toga made from a bed sheet and a heavy steel sword.

But now, with the initiation ceremonies stamped out, Randy's once-proud Roman toga was nothing more than a silly-looking bed sheet again.

He clenched his teeth, drew his sword, and began thrashing it against a huge steel post in the center of the room.

"Damn! Damn! Damn!" Randy shouted. "It's not fair! How can he do this! This place ain't what is used to be!"

August 31

With all the drug scandals going on in professional sports these days, it came as no surprise when a representative from the NFL's Drug Enforcement Division came in today and lectured the team on drug abuse. "If you are doing drugs," he warned, "you will get caught."

One method of "catching" drug abusers is with spot urinalysis tests. This system has been adopted by several schools, including Auburn. We do not have such a system, but after today, I'll bet it's coming.

The NFL's drug agent asked us to close our eyes and put our heads on our desks while he took an informal poll.

"How many of you here have used or tried marijuana?" he asked.

I could hear the rustle of several arms going up.

"OK," the man said, "how many of you have used or are using cocaine?"

I listened closer, but heard nothing.

"Come on, now," the man urged, "this is strictly confidential. We're not going to go running to your coaches. . . . .anybody using cocaine?"

Again, I heard nothing.

Doug Vickers and Walter Lewis stood beside the "drug man" and counted the hands.

After the meeting, I asked Doug how many had raised their hands. He wouldn't tell me.

"But," he said, "I *was* surprised."

College athletes are not naive. We read the papers and we

know where the coaches are coming from. We also realize that a lot of kids look up to us as role models, and we try to not do anything to tarnish that image. But there will always be exceptions. Players who use drugs are going to use them, and players who make a friendly wager now and then are going to gamble. And when they are caught, we all suffer with them.

September 2

Of all the rotten luck. . .I was diving for a pass in a scrimmage today and landed on my shoulder. Now, if I make any fast moves, it feels like a knife stabbing me in the neck. This is one injury that's going to be tough to hide from the coaches.

Otherwise, the scrimmage was great. I caught a 75-yard touchdown pass from Walter Lewis on the second play of the game and we beat the third unit 52-6. The defense stopped us only once and we had zero turnovers. This was Alabama football at its best. But if I hadn't hurt my shoulder, I'd feel a lot better about it.

One sports writer everyone tries to avoid is Don Kausler of the *Birmingham News*. Don has been on the team's official "S" list since last season when he wrote that our schedule looked like "Disney on Parade."

Since then, no player wants to grant him an interview. If we see him standing on the field after a practice, we'll walk 50 yards out of our way just to slip past him. If we see him standing near the entrance to Bryant Hall, we'll sneak through another door. But because he's always hanging around, it's hard to avoid him all the time. Sometimes, he just seems to pop up out of nowhere. One of those times was today.

I was coming off the field, worrying about my shoulder, when he appeared in front of me. He was working on a story about what might happen if Walter Lewis got hurt. I could tell he didn't think much of our depth at quarterback, and wanted me to say, "We'd fall flat on our face!" And although I may have thought it, I didn't want to say it—least of all in the newspaper! I gave him a bunch of innocuous quotes about how great Walter ran the option last year, and how quickly Mike Shula is coming along. Kausler still wasn't satisfied. He frowned and asked the question again—only in a different way. So, I rephrased my answer, threw in more innocuous quotes, and waited for his reaction. He scribbled down my reply on his note pad, said "Thanks," and moved on to other unsuspecting players.

September 3

Woke up today and my shoulder was so swollen that I could hardly lift my arm. There was no getting around it this time—I *had* to tell Coach Goostree. He gave me some pills to fight inflammation and packed my shoulder in ice.

I didn't practice today, and "Goose" says I won't practice again until he is convinced that I am all right.

Looks like I'm going to have to summon up my acting skills again. . .

September 4

We were sitting in the projection room today when Coach Perkins walked in carrying the *Birmingham News* sports section in his hand.

"Remember what I said about the press?" he asked as he glared around the room. It was one of those type of questions that required no answer.

"I said to watch what you said to the press," he went on. "Now, I'm not picking on anybody, but this story (he thumped the newspaper for emphasis) is an example of what I've been trying to get at. . ."

He unfolded the paper and held it up. I could see that it was Don Kausler's story on what we would do if Walter Lewis got hurt. "Oh, no," I thought, "somebody has said something bad about Mike Shula or Paul Fields." I sat back and waited for the storm.

Perkins adjusted his glasses and frowned.

"Here," he said, "I'll read you some of it:

"Without Lewis, however, some of the pieces of Alabama's wide-open offense would be missing.

"I guess we'd be a little more basic. We probably wouldn't use the option as much. . ."

A cold chill rushed through me. *I* said that! That was *me* talking!

My hands began trembling. I tried to act nonchalant, but couldn't. Instead, I was blushing as I slid lower into my seat. I hoped that this would be the end of it.

It wasn't. Coach Perkins scanned the room with that cold, icy glare in his eyes, finally resting them on me. Squirming in my seat, I looked away. Now, I was *praying* that he had finished.

But Perkins kept right on.

"Know who said that?" he asked accusingly. "One of our seniors said that."

Oh, God, no! This can't be happening!

"Joey Jones said that!"

All eyes turned on me. My heart was pounding so hard I could hear it beating in my ear drums.

The whole thing lasted only a couple of seconds, but it seemed to stretch into a lifetime.

"Now, this is not that bad," Perkins finally said. "Georgia Tech probably already knows that we were going to run the option anyway. But that's just an example of what I've been trying to tell you about—watching what you say to the press."

September 5

I got a new nickname today—"Game Day Boy."

That's what they call players who don't practice all week but play when game day rolls around. Major Ogilvie was a "Game Day Boy." He would have a great game, but would be so sore or banged up that he couldn't practice all the next week. Then, he'd get well just in time for the next game. I'm sure it wasn't Major's fault. Sometimes, it just works out that way.

So, today, I stood on the sideline wearing that stupid yellow jersey and wondering if the coaches think I'm faking.

"When you gonna take off that yellow jersey and play some football, 'Game Day Boy'?" they'd ask.

Or somebody else would say, "You trying to win the Major Ogilvie Award?"

I hate it on the sidelines. the players make me feel guilty when I know there's absolutely no reason to feel guilty. I've only missed four days' practice in four years. But when I'm hurt, I know it.

I was so shaken up at being accused of giving away team secrets at yesterday's meeting, I failed to mention what the meeting was about. It was about Georgia Tech.

Each Sunday before a game we receive a chart, breaking down the next opponent's tendencies—things they characteristically do in certain situations.

For example:

Do they blitz on third down? Do they blitz on second down? On third-and-four, do they run or do they pass?

In addition, we receive a list of all players returning from last year along with a report of their statistics. We also receive a chart of a football field, showing which positions on the field Tech is most likely to pass from, and another chart showing their various defensive coverages or so forth.

The actual game plan isn't handed out until Tuesday or Wednesday, depending on when game film arrives in the mail. Once the coaches view that, they will set up a game plan, which is really nothing more than a list of plays that we will run that week. Then, it's just a matter of matching up the offensive play that works against a certain defense. Sometimes, situations in a game will force you to alter your game plan, but that's rare. You always try to stick to your game plan because that's what you've worked on all week.

Of course, you never see any game films during the week of the season-opener, unless you review films of last year's game (or if the opponent opened a week early). So, our "tendency reports" on Tech became more valuable than ever.

Coach Rutledge thinks he did us a big favor by letting us have freshman skits tonight. Believe me, it was no favor. The skits were terrible. These freshmen can't do anything right.

September 6

Now that the Georgia Tech game is just four days away, I take this opportunity to educate you on some of the words and phrases that often pop up in conversation around the dressing room or dorm.

For example:

A quarterback who has a *soft touch* throws passes that are

easy to catch.

Bullets are passes thrown so hard that they bounce off a receiver's chest.

A *wounded duck* is a badly-thrown pass that wobbles in the air. When a defensive back sees a *wounded duck*, he pretends to aim an imaginary rifle and yells, "Pow! Pow! Pow!"

A defensive back who *plays soft* is one who lines up eight to ten yards off the line of scrimmage. If he gets any farther back than that, he is said to be *out of play.*

A defensive back who gets closer than eight yards from the line of scrimmage has *nose trouble,* or is simply a *nosey player.*

A quarterback *threads the needle* if he completes a pass between two defensive backs.

A receiver who makes great catches is said to have *good hands.*

A receiver who drops too many passes is said to have *hands of stone.*

A receiver who drops passes because he's afraid of getting hit is *hearing footsteps.*

Red Territory is the area between the 20-yard line and the goal line. When you reach *red territory*, you're supposed to score.

A *post* is a pass pattern that extends 15 yards down field, then angles toward the goal post.

A *flag* is a pass route that angles toward the small flags at each end of the goal line.

Outs are routes that break quickly to the sidelines.

Ins are routes that break across the middle of the field.

When a lineman tells a quarterback or running back to stay out of the *fire*, he's talking about the congested area in the middle of the line where all the hard hitting is taking place.

Fire is also what you yell when something goes wrong on long snap situations, such as punts or field goal attempts.

When a touchdown is scored, a player may yell, *"that's six!"*

When a pass is intercepted, a player yells, *"Bingo!"*

And when a punt is too short to be fielded by the specialty team, they will shout, *"Peter! Peter! Peter!"* The suggestion there is that football players, being of the male gender, will avoid "a peter" and run the opposite way.

Coach Campbell, however, once considered changing the "peter" call.

"I don't know if we should use that one or not," he said. "Some of you boys may not run away from a peter!"

Ah, football. . .there's nothing like it.

September 7

I know how Paul Carruth feels about being left out of everything. I didn't practice yesterday, and I didn't practice today. The rest of the team is out there working on plays for Georgia Tech, and I'm stuck on the sidelines. It's a miserable feeling.

The campus is turning into Reportersville, U.S.A. again. You see reporters hanging around the dorm every morning and in the cafeteria every afternoon. Seems that Alabama's first season without Coach Bryant is really big news. I heard that John Underwood of *Sports Illustrated* has been following Coach Perkins around all week. Underwood is the one who co-authored Coach Bryant's biography, *Bear*. Maybe I can ask him for some tips on my book.

Big meeting tonight. We had our first real pre-game meeting with Coach Perkins, and I was surprised at how loose and relaxed he was. Instead of frowning and glaring at people, he was laughing and cracking jokes. Maybe the pressure is getting to him?

Coach Perkins tells us that he is good friends with Georgia Tech coach Bill Curry. He says that they were roommates in the pros. He also says that Bill Curry knows his football and is doing everything possible to make Tech a winning team.

"I've seen the films when Tech beat us two years ago," Coach Perkins said. "And I saw a team get beat that never in a million years should've been beaten by that team. I want to make sure that never happens again. You are a better team than they are, and you've got to go out there and win these games you are supposed to win. That's what championship teams do."

Championship teams? Hmmm, I like the sound of that.

For three nights now, the third floor of Bryant Hall has been overwhelmed with the sound of the theme song from the movie *Rocky*. The record will play through at least twice, and sometimes as many as three times.

So, when the music started again tonight, I followed the sound—all the way next door to Randy Edwards' room.

"Why in the world do you play that record every night?" I asked.

"Because I like it," he said. "Besides, it fires me up. It makes me *hun-gry!*"

"OK," I said "I admit it does get the old heart pumping and the juices flowing, but to play it every night over and over again? Doesn't it lose its effectiveness after awhile?"

"Naw," he said," I only play it on special occasions."

"So what's the special occasion?" I asked.

"Georgia Tech!"

Good practice today. No, better make that great practice today.

Coach Goostree finally cleared me to return to action, and it felt great to get back out there and get the kinks out. My shoulder is still a little sore, but it's nothing I can't stand. Anything beats standing on the sidelines in that yellow jersey. Was beginning to worry that "Goose" was going to keep me out of the game Saturday.

After practice, we were treated to another pep talk from Joe Namath, only this seemed more like an endorsement of Coach Perkins.

"You've got a good man here coaching you," Namath said. "Coach Bryant knew what he was doing when he chose Ray Perkins for this job. He couldn't have gotten a better man.

"I know Ray real well, and he's going to do you right. So you guys need to go out there Saturday and play for him just as you would Coach Bryant. Go out there and play like Alabama has always played, and win this game."

September 9
Bessemer

The butterflies are fluttering here again at the Oak Tree Inn. They always do at this time of year.

This is our traditional resting place on Friday nights before games at Legion Field. This is where we come to relax, to get away from all the noise of the Friday night fraternity parties.

The University could save hundreds of dollars by busing the team into Birmingham on Saturday mornings, but Coach Bryant always felt this arrangement was best for all concerned. And with his Legion Field record of 68 wins, 15 losses and five ties, nobody was about to argue.

But even these familiar surroundings seem odd without Coach Bryant here running things. Come to think of it, the whole day has been rather peculiar.

It is almost as if our entire itinerary has been a bizarre attempt at leaving things just as Coach Bryant had left them. As always, today's practice was nothing more than a short, 45-minute walk-through of plays. After that, we had our usual dinner in Bryant Hall. At 6:45 p.m., we began boarding the team buses. At five minutes before seven, Coach Perkins stepped onto the bus, carrying a newspaper just as Coach Bryant always did on bus trips. Coach Perkins looked around the bus and sat down in what used to be Coach Bryant's favorite seat—front row, right side. Directly across from him sat Coach Goostree in his usual place, also reading the paper. Nothing had changed. Well, almost nothing.

Once we reached the hotel, however, the similarities ceased.

Whereas Coach Bryant would always send us out to a movie, Coach Perkins held a team meeting. We could have done without that.

"I don't see why we can't go to a movie," Mike White, our resident movie buff, grumbled as we carried our bags to our rooms. "What can we possibly learn tonight that we don't already know? Heck, if we don't know it by now, we might as well hang it up."

But that's Coach Perkins for you. He says the 24 hours before the game are the most important, that this is when the mind is more alert and more receptive to mental preparation for the game. He says the more people we can get to thinking about the game tonight and how they will carry out their assignments tomorrow, the greater our chances will be for success. That may be true for some players, but not for all.

Some players get so wound up before a game that they need a few hours away from football. For those, movie night was the answer. The movies gave them an outlet for that pent-up nervousness and anxiety. It offered a chance to unwind, to get the kinks out after a long bus trip, and to get fresh air.

It's not that the movie selection was so socially redeeming that we would otherwise be culturally deprived by not seeing them. It's the principle of the thing. In fact, we very rarely saw an entire movie anyway because we always arrived late. Still, it gave you a good feeling to walk into that darkened theatre and see all the heads turn and listen to the whispers, "That's the football team! That's *Alabama!*" It made you feel important, confident. And with a game coming up, that's nothing to be snickered at.

A lot of times you could see people gazing through the darkness in search of the man in the houndstooth hat. But Coach Bryant and the assistant coaches always stayed back at the hotel. The only "chaperone" we had was Coach Goostree. And we kept him hopping.

With four movies running concurrently, we could choose whichever movie we wanted to see. This, of course, caused real problems for Coach Goostree. The only way he could make certain no one was about to whisk away some wide-eyed school girl was by spending a few minutes in each theatre. Even that had its drawbacks. More times than not, "Goose" would stroll into the theatre, plop down in a seat, and look up at the screen only to see a nude couple in an R-rated bedroom scene. "Goose" would turn 15 shades of crimson and then jump up and leave the theatre muttering to himself. The next day we would tease him about it.

But houndstooth hats and Friday nights at the movies are things of the past now. Like they say, it's the dawn of a new era. And Coach Perkins is determined to start that era with a win.

"Make it *mean* something to you," he said at the meeting. "From a mental standpoint, don't think of it as just being the first of 12 games (notice how he included the bowl game in there?). Don't think of Tech as your first game—think of them as your last game. Make it *mean* something. Make it count."

Everybody asks if I am superstitious. The answer is, "Yes—very."

When we arrive at the stadium tomorrow, I'll make a ritual out of getting dressed. Everything has to be just right.

I'm especially picky about my shoes. If they are all white and clean, I won't wear them. Clean, white shoes are distracting. My shoes have to be all scuffed up, stained and dirty. If they aren't, I'll take them outside and beat them against the ground until they look six months old.

I also have a pair of lucky socks. They are old and tattered, but they're comfortable. Without them, I'm useless. Joe Henley, one of our managers who has since graduated, always made it a point to see that I had them. But once before a game at Bryant-Denny Stadium, I looked into my locker and couldn't find them.

"Hey, Joe!" I yelled. "Where are my lucky socks?"

Joe slapped his palm against his forehead. "Oh, no!" he cried. "I'm sorry—I forgot 'em. I'll go get them."

Before I could tell him not to bother, Joe had rushed out the door, jumped into a truck, and was speeding off toward the Coliseum to retrieve my lucky socks from the equipment room.

Five minutes later, Joe returned with my lucky socks.

"I can't let you go out there without your secret weapon," he said and smiled.

So, I went out and caught four passes for 80 yards and we beat Vanderbilt 24-21. Joe had saved the day.

Another habit I have is wearing wrist bands over my elbows, a quirk that drives Coach Goostree crazy. He keeps insisting that I wear elbow pads to protect me from turf burns, but elbow pads are much too cumbersome and they restrict flexibility. Also, instead of wearing wrist bands over my wrists, I wrap adhesive tape around them just tight enough that my fingertips tingle. I feel this gives my hands more sensitivity when trying to catch the ball. Another little trick is wrapping the tape inside out so that the sticky side faces outward. This way, the ball sticks when it touches my wrists.

I'm not sure why I wear eye black except that people say it shields light from your eyes when you're looking for the ball. I can't tell that it does anything. But every game, I've got to have that eye black on there.

Knee pads are another matter. If I could get away with it. I wouldn't wear any at all. Neither would any of the other receivers. Knee pads restrict your movements, slow you down, and are like running on three legs. Jesse Bendross hates them so much that he will hitch his pants up to his rib cage before practices. And for games, Jesse (who is four inches taller and 20 pounds heavier than I) will wear the same size pants I do just to keep the knee pads riding above his knees.

Of course, exposing the knee this way increases the risk of injury by 100 percent. But if a receiver could choose between something that would guarantee him 10 catches a game but may ruin his knee for life, he would choose the catches every time.

Linemen have their own tricks of the trade. They will tape their jerseys to their shoulder pads to keep opposing linemen from pulling them down. And they will tie their jersey sleeves in knots, tuck them underneath their pads and tape them under. Everyone is looking for that edge.

I'm looking for that edge when I refuse to tie my shoe laces before I walk onto the field because it might bring bad luck. I'm looking for that edge when I massage my temples with ice cubes before each game because I think it will help me see the ball better. And I'm looking for that edge when I count my steps when running from the huddle to the line of scrimmage. All steps must be taken in multiples of five—five, ten, fifteen—or, I'm convinced something terrible will happen on the play. So, if I reach the line of scrimmage in twelve steps, I'll stamp my feet three more times just to be on the safe side.

Like the poem says, "It's All in a State of Mind."

My roomie on Friday night during the season is Paul Fields. I'm lucky to have him.

I'm lousy company on Fridays because that's when my game face goes on. I started this morning by not going to class. I had classes from 9 a.m. until 1 p.m., but I kept finding excuses not to go. This is not unusual for me. I never go to class on Fridays before a game. It's just asking too much of my brain to think football *and* finance with a game coming up. All my feelings and thoughts are geared to the game. Nothing else matters. By Friday night, I'm as moody an introvert as you will ever see. It's get serious or get out.

That's where Paul Fields comes in. Paul helps out by keep-me posted on what is discussed in the quarterback meeting. And tonight, Paul tells me that I shouldn't concern myself with catching a bunch of passes tomorrow.

"You can forget about going deep tomorrow," Paul said. "Coach Perkins wants to run the ball."

"All the time?" I asked, not without some disappointment.

"Well, no, but just about every pass is going to be off of play action. We'll be dumping off to the tight ends mostly."

"Darn!" I said. "Well, so much for the passing show everybody is expecting."

Ordinarily, Paul would not have received all this information until Saturday morning—at least, that's when Coach Bryant had his meeting with the quarterbacks. He would adjourn the regular team meeting by saying, "I want to take a walk with the quarterbacks." Then, they would take a leisurely stroll around the hotel grounds talking about whatever came to mind.

"You know what I miss, J.J.?" Paul said.

"What's that?"

"More than anything, I'm going to miss that walk with Coach Bryant."

September 10
Bryant Hall

Opening Day for some—opening day for me. There *is* a difference you know.

I had forgotten what season openers were like, but it didn't take long to refresh my memory. Football can be very hazardous to your mental health.

When you play well but the team loses, you feel guilty. When you play badly but the team wins, you *still* feel guilty. The only way you can come out of a game feeling good about yourself is when *everything* goes perfectly—both for the team *and* for you.

Tonight, I feel guilty.

We beat Georgia Tech 20-7 and although I'm thankful for that, I got off to a very poor start. I failed to see a strong safety blitz in the second quarter and because of that, Jack Westbrooke burst through the line and almost took Walter Lewis' head off. Fortunately, Walter was not hurt and managed to dump the ball off to Joe Carter just in time. The worst to come of it was that Joe was held to one-yard gain and I got my butt chewed out by Coach Rader on the sidelines.

"Why the heck didn't you pick up that blitz?!" he yelled.

"Er uh. . .I'm sorry, Coach. I just didn't see it."

"Didn't see it?! You better start seeing it! Walter might get sacked for a big loss next time!"

"Yes sir, Coach."

He was right, of course, my mistake *could* have cost us dearly. But there won't be a "next time." I'll make certain of that.

I can't understand how I screwed up like that in the first place. But as I said before, it just wasn't my day. For some reason, I spent half the afternoon daydreaming and I couldn't shake the feeling for the life of me. Nothing seemed real—not the noise, not the game, nothing. I moved in slow motion, and when somebody spoke to me, I didn't hear them. I almost got hit in the head with a ball once during pre-game warm-up because I wasn't paying attention.

I thought about Coach Bryant a lot, too. That was expected, but also unavoidable. When Coach Perkins asked for a moment of silence before the game "for someone who is very dear to us," we knew exactly who he was talking about. When I pulled my helmet down from the locker and saw the hounds-tooth hat decal on the back, a cold chill raced down my spine. I got that same feeling again when I walked near the north end zone goal post before the game.

But the most peculiar feeling of all was watching Coach Perkins during the game. Since I had never seen him actually coaching, I didn't know what to expect. I do now, and it looks as if it could be a long, long season because, once he gets out there on that field, he turns into a total stranger. And he seems to prefer it that way.

Everything revolves around him and him alone. It's like he's out there all by himself and we're just pawns to be positioned and moved around. He lives and dies with every play, jumping into the air on the great plays and cringing and cussing on the bad ones. And when a penalty flag goes against us, his eyes bulge like ping pong balls and blood rushes to his face. He is obsessed with the game; with winning it.

There was no idle small talk the way there was with Coach Bryant—he was much too busy for that. And if you screwed up (the way I did), he wouldn't even acknowledge you as you ran to the sidelines, or if he did, it's just a quick, icy glare.

Coach Perkins is big on organization, too. When Pat Dye made his debut at Auburn, the newspapers were filled with stories about how disorganized the coaches were on the sidelines. That certainly wasn't the case today. If anything, it was *too* organized.

With most of the assistant coaches calling plays or setting up defenses from the press box, there was more room on the sidelines. But Coach Perkins used up all the extra space by pacing up and down the sidelines and whipping the cord to his headset around. There was no milling around, either. You had a certain place to stand and you had better be there. It took some of the fun out of it. I used to enjoy standing close to Coach Bryant when the defense was on the field just to hear what he had to say. But with Coach Perkins, I could never get far enough away.

Don't get me wrong. I'm not faulting Coach Perkins for his behavior, only describing it. Heck, I'm just glad that he is so involved in the game. If he had been out there daydreaming the way I was, we probably would have lost today.

The game was not a great game as games go. First of all, it was hot as blazes. It was 124 degrees on the artificial turf all through the day; emergency carts circled the stadium with their sirens whining as they hauled off fans who had gotten too much sun. It got to the players, too. Mike Travis, the cornerback who was covering me most of the afternoon, once ran to the Tech sideline and collapsed.

All in all, it was a typical season opener. We fumbled the ball five times and lost it once, that one coming when Craig "Touchdown" Turner made his patented dive over the top of the pile at the goal line late in the game. We should have scored then, but we should have scored other times too.

Our ballyhooed offense just didn't click today—or at least as well as I think it is capable. We only got 159 yards rushing, and Walter completed 10 of 19 passes for 204 yards. He was only intercepted once. But it still wasn't the passing show everyone was expecting. I only caught one pass for 26 yards and then had to explain (with great diplomacy) to all the reporters why "one of the main weapons in Alabama's new pro-set offense" was not utilized.

This game was played in a fish bowl. Everyone had come to see what the new Tide was like. They wanted to see the man who followed Coach Bryant. and they wanted to see this new high-powered offense. Now that they have their answers, maybe we can get down to playing football again without all that extra weight on our shoulders.

And so, with victory No. 1 secured, we piled onto the bus and headed back to Tuscaloosa, yelling and screaming like a bunch of high school kids. All except me, that is. I was too busy brooding about the strong safety blitz.

September 11

The bad part of waking up on Sunday is remembering what you did on Saturday. And all I could think about this morning was that stupid strong safety blitz that I missed.

The more I thought about it, the worse it became. I started wondering if Coach Perkins had lost faith in me. I wondered if I had blown my chance; if Coach Perkins felt that I could never be the clutch player he wanted me to be.

I kept seeing the play over and over in my head. Even as I drove over to the Coliseum to watch films of the game, I kept thinking, "He probably thinks I'll never get that strong safety blitz right."

By the time I reached the double doors to the projection room, I was a walking basket case. That's when I felt a hand on my shoulder. It was Billy Getchel, the walk on. He hadn't made the traveling roster, but he had gone to see the game.

"Hey, man, what happened on that blitz yesterday?" he asked.

"Oh, I just didn't see it," I said.

"Didn't see it!" he said, sounding surprised. "Man, I was in the stands and I saw it!"

"Oh, gee thanks Billy," I said. "That makes me feel much better."

So I sat there in the projection room, dreading the moment when Coach Henshaw would flip on the projector and I would see that foul up all over again. Most likely, he would show the play twice—once in slow motion.

But it wasn't half as bad as I expected. Coach Henshaw did run through the play twice, but all he said to me was, "Joey, I believe we've talked to you about this before. We know you know what to do, but you've got to start paying attention to what's going on in the backfield."

Actually, it was quite painless. But that's the way it usually is when you win. Win a game, and watching game films is like watching the Keystone Kops in action. Mistakes are laughed off. But when you lose, if you have your foot planted in the wrong direction, the coaches will crawl your butt. The only sound you hear then is the projector clicking away and the coaches cussing.

Craig Turner wasn't as lucky. His fumble on the goal line didn't go over very well with Coach Henshaw.

"You know better than to jump up there like that, Craig!" he said. "That's the kind of play that you've got to jump up there and roll over with the ball so if they hit anything at all, it won't be the ball. You can't let them get up under you and hit the ball! You should know that—you did it all last year!"

Craig just hung his head down and mumbled, "Yes, sir. Yes, sir."

I know how he feels. It wasn't that great a day for me either. I graded 80 percent, but I was awarded no "winning plays" and the missed safety blitz was considered a critical error.

What all this means is that I didn't grade out as "a winner." And losers don't get to eat from the training table. This is the first time I've missed training table in two years, but I deserved it. So, while all the "winners" are feasting on T-bone steaks, baked potatoes, shrimp, tossed salads and banana splits all week, I'll be dining on junk like liver and blackeyed peas. *Yeech!*

The really tough part about football is that as soon as one game is over, there's another one staring you right in the face. It's like being the gunslinger in the old westerns—there's always somebody waiting to gun you down.

The challenger this week is Ole Miss. Usually we look upon the Rebels as just a good team to scrimmage against. We always beat them easily. In fact, Alabama has lost only two games to Ole Miss since a 0-0 tie in 1933.

But Ole Miss is getting tired of being our whipping boy, and they've cancelled our contract with them until 1988. This both amuses and disappoints me. I can't blame them, but I sure do hate to see the series end. This could also give Ole Miss players an extra incentive to beat us. And since they are now 0-2 already after losing 37-17 to Memphis State and 27-23 to Tulane, they are bound to play loose against us.

Saw the first "Alabama Football Review" today. It was. . . well, different.

Whereas Coach Bryant opened his Sunday afternoon television show with a peaceful scene of Denny Chimes, Coach Perkins' show opens with highlights from the Liberty Bowl. The theme music is different, too. Instead of those macho voices booming out the old-fashioned rendition of "Yea, Alabama!," you hear a modern snappy instrumental version that sounds like something Doc Severenson's band would play between station breaks on the "Tonight Show."

The show has also been cut from an hour to thirty minutes. And because of that, the exchange between Coach Perkins and sportscaster Mike Hogewood is very fast paced.

It goes something like this:

Hogewood: "Welcome to the Alabama Football Review! Good win, Coach!"

Perkins: "Thanks, Mike. I'm glad we won."

Hogewood: "Me too! Let's watch."

Flash to 12 minutes of game footage.

Flash back to Hogewood.

Hogewood: "That's the first half! Now for a word from our sponsors!"

Flash to Coach Perkins catching a bag of Frito Lay corn chips.

Flash to Mike Hogewood.

Hogewood: "Let's watch the second half!"

Perkins: "OK."

Flash to 10 minutes of game footage.

Flash to Hogewood.

Hogewood: "That's it! See you next week."

Of course, that's an exaggeration. But you get the idea.

I'm sure this change in format is an attempt to usher in the new era and give the show a slicker look. But in doing so, I think they lost some of the magic that was the "Bear Bryant Show."

September 12

Walked into the cafeteria last night and was overcome by the aroma of T-bone steaks. My mouth began watering and my stomach growling, but then I remembered I hadn't made the training table. Instead, I had a choice between chicken pot pie or Beanie Weenies. I choked down half my pot pie, then went out and got myself a Big Mac.

Another reminder that college football isn't just a game: Walter Lewis is nursing a slightly sprained ankle, Joe Carter has a bruised knee, and four linebackers—Todd Roper, Jimmy Watts, Scott McRae and Emmanuel King—are suffering from a variety of ailments.

Remember. . ."no pain, no gain."

September 14

Now that the season is under way, several players have begun sprouting beards. Most of the linemen have them—Randy Edwards, John McIntosh, Joe Dismuke, Hardy Walker.

Mike Adcock was trying to grow one, too, but wasn't having much success. The next thing I knew, he had shaved it off.

"Why did you shave off your beard?" I asked him.

"Because I walked up to Coach Perkins the other day to ask him a question. But in the middle of my sentence, he reached into his pocket, pulled out a dollar and held it under my nose."

"I asked him, 'What's this for?' And he said, 'Go buy yourself a razor.' I didn't know whether he was kidding me or not, but I shaved it off just to be on the safe side."

That's right, team, you heard right. It's perfectly OK to grow full beards—so long as you grow them overnight.

Sitting in the classroom today I noticed I am blind as a bat. Actually, I already knew this but didn't want to admit it. So, I whipped out my eye glasses just long enough to see what was written on the board and copy down the notes.

And immediately, everyone around me started asking questions:

"You wear glasses?!"

"Yes, but only when I have to."

"When did you start wearing glasses?"

"Two weeks ago. Mom got tired of me squinting and forced me to go to the eye doctor."

"But can you still see the football?"

"Footballs are no problem—just tiny writing on blackboards."

I pulled the glasses off and vowed to never wear them in public again.

Coach Perkins is a man of few words—one and a half words to be exact. Those words are "Standpoint" and "wise," the latter being a suffix which may attach to any noun, pronoun or verb.

Example:

At tonight's team meeting, I tried to keep count of the number of times he used the word "standpoint" and how many times he used the suffix "-wise." I lost count at 18 "standpoints" and 13 "-wises."

So, a typical speech from Coach Perkins sounds something like: "From a preparation standpoint and from a coaching standpoint, I am pleased with the progress we've made in practice this week. But from an offensive standpoint, there's still room for improvement. We've simply got to get better from an execution standpoint. Talent-wise and ability-wise, I know we can match up with anybody. Execution-wise, we've got to improve."

You might say that from a player's standpoint, Coach Perkins is a "-wise" guy.

September 15

Had a great practice today. I made one great leaping catch, a good diving catch, and another sideline catch where I dragged my foot just inside the boundary before falling out. Best of all, though, I've got that strong safety blitz down to a science. I haven't missed a blitz all week.

Coach Perkins appears to be enjoying himself more this week, too. He isn't frowning half as much as last week and he is much more patient. He will never admit it, but he must be as relieved as we are to get that first game out of the way.

News flash: Southwestern Louisiana has been named to replace Ole Miss on our schedule next season. I've always said that there are no such things as guaranteed wins, but this has to be one heckuva safe bet.

If I don't get back on the training table soon, I'm going to be nothing more than skin and bones. I've dropped five pounds just this week because I can't work up an appetite for what they're serving. It's hard to get excited over corn, creamed potatoes and mystery meat.

What's mystery meat you ask?

It's not beef. It's not pork. It's not even fish or poultry.

It *is* a mystery.

It's crazy, I know, but I hear there will be representatives from the Blue-Gray All-Star Game and the Sugar Bowl at Saturday's game with Ole Miss. I guess they know championship material when they see it, huh?

September 16

Cut all my classes again today. This is a terrible habit, but a fellow has to keep his priorities in order, you know.

My game face is more obvious than I thought.

"Got that game face on again huh, Joey," Mike Adcock said today. "You gotta loosen up some kid. Have a little fun. It's only a game."

Mike, by the way, is a game captain tomorrow.

Even at home games you can't stay at home. There are just too many fraternity houses and too many parties going on around Bryant Hall. So, we load up the buses again and head to this hotel about five miles from campus.

Of course, there were no movies again tonight—just another team meeting. But, from a preparation standpoint and a listening standpoint, it was pretty good meeting-wise.

Coach Perkins reminded us that we are the team that blew our 56-game winning streak in Bryant-Denny Stadium by losing to Southern Miss last year. "And," Perkins said, "you are the ones who can start that streak going again starting right here tomorrow. This is it, this is No. 1."

When Paul Fields returned to the room after the quarterback meeting tonight, I asked him, "What's it look like for tomorrow? Are we going to do a lot of passing?"

For once, Paul acted like he didn't want to answer.

"Well, yeah," Paul said. "We're going to try to pass on them."

"Great!" I said. "I'm going to get some long ones at last, huh?"

"Well. . ." Paul replied. "Yes and no. Coach Perkins says that if we throw the ball long, he wants to try to get the ball to Greg Richardson."

"Greg Richardson?! Why Greg Richardson? What's wrong with me? I can catch the long passes too!"

"I know," said Paul, "But Coach Perkins likes Greg's speed. He says Greg has got 'a little something in his back pocket!' "

"Something in his back pocket?" I repeated. "What's that mean?"

"I'm not sure," said Paul. "I suppose it means that he has an extra burst of speed."

"And I suppose he thinks I'm slow," I said, shaking my head. "I tell you, Paul, sometimes I can't figure these coaches out. Here, I've been begging Coach Felker all summer to send me out for the long passes but all he would say was, 'Don't worry, you'll get your chance.'

"And now that we are going to throw deep, they think a freshman can do the job better than I can. I just can't figure these coaches out at all."

September 17

Now *that's* more like it.

We won 40 to nothing. I caught three passes for 39 yards and didn't miss a single blitz, and the defense not only got a shutout but scored a safety as well. This is the way football is supposed to be played.

The offense executed so well that we were able to play three quarterbacks. Walter Lewis played only the first half and the first series of the third quarter, but completed 13 of 15 passes for 230 yards to break Ken Stabler's single game pass percentage completion record. After that, Paul Fields came in and finished out the third quarter and Mike Shula played the fourth quarter.

If I have any complaints at all, it's that my ankle hurts like the devil. During the second quarter, I turned my ankle while blocking for Ricky Moore and I spent the rest of the game watching from the sidelines with my foot in an ice bucket. But it doesn't hurt half as bad when you're winning.

September 18

Woke up today and my ankle was black and blue from the tips of my toes to the back of my heel. So, I limped over to the training room and Coach Goostree soaked my ankle in a bucket of ice and gave me some pills to keep the swelling down.

"Looks bad," he said, "Come back at 1 o'clock."

So, I went back at 1 o'clock and put more ice on it.

"Doesn't look much better, does it?" Coach Goostree said. "Stop back by after the team meeting."

So I went to the team meeting, reviewed game films, and found out that I graded 93 percent against Ole Miss and could now sit at the training table. I felt better all ready.

Afterwards, I went back to the training room for another 45 minutes of Coach Goostree's miracle ice treatments. He still wasn't satisfied.

"Better stay off that ankle today," he said. "Go back and keep it elevated. Come back at 9 tonight."

"At 9???" I said. "Do I have to?"

"Yes, you have to. You want to get well, don't you?"

"Well, yeah. . .but does this mean I can't practice tomorrow?"

"Probably, but we'll see about that tomorrow."

See what I mean? When you're hurt, you're hurt.

Next up is Vanderbilt. Vandy is 1-1 after beating Iowa State 29-26 on a 10-yard touchdown pass with seven seconds left in yesterday's game. I used to think of Vanderbilt as just a bunch of smart guys who couldn't play football, while we were just a bunch of dumb rednecks who couldn't do anything *but* play football. But if they were so smart, why couldn't they play football? I didn't have the answer for that, and apparently, they didn't either because we would usually beat them to a pulp. But now, since George MacIntyre took over as coach, Vandy has become a very good football team and they seem to get better every year.

Coach Steve Hale, who prepared the scouting report on the Commodores (also known as Commies or Commodes), says they are as good or better than last year. Their offense, as usual, is wide open—Kurt Page threw 49 times in the season-opening loss to Maryland. and their defense is experienced with people like Karl Jordan, Steve Bearden and Leonard Coleman coming back. I've been playing against Coleman for three years now and I know what he can do to a receiver. I rank him up there as one of the best defensive backs in the Southeastern Conference. Free safety Manuel Young broke his leg against Maryland and will be out for six weeks. That's a bad break for Manuel but a lucky break for us. I remember my sophomore year when Manuel drove us crazy by making tackles all over the field. He was everywhere.

So, Vandy is improving all the time. Their old image as a perennial loser is undeserved now. And if we don't realize that, we could be in a heap of trouble next weekend.

Tsk. Tsk. Just read that Auburn lost 20-7 to Texas in a nationally televised game yesterday. Welcome to the big time, boys.

September 19

Put on my silly little yellow jersey again today and watched everybody else have a good time at practice. I was standing on the sidelines feeling sorry for myself when Coach Perkins walked over.

"You're gonna make it aren't you?" he asked.

"Yes, sir. Tomorrow or Wednesday."

"Well, let's not push for tomorrow, but we'll see what we can do about Wednesday."

You know, he's really not such a bad guy.

I'm not the only one in pain these days. Roosevelt Hill, an inside linebacker from Newnan, Georgia, tore his knee apart in the Ole Miss game. I went by to see him in the hospital tonight and he looked terrible. His knee was swollen the size of a balloon, and Roosevelt said that the knee was ripped totally out of the socket along with every cartilage. They'll operate on him tomorrow.

"Looks like this is it for me," Roosevelt said. "I can kiss my career goodbye."

I hate to see this happen to Roosevelt. The coaches decided not to renew his scholarship a couple of years ago, but Roosevelt stayed, worked hard and earned the scholarship back as well as a starting position. He's a fighter, but injuries such as this are something you can't fight.

Made my return to the training table tonight. Not only is the food (steak, of course) better, but so is the conversation.

We were conversing on Auburn's misfortune of losing to Texas 20-7 when someone came up with this gem.

"Did you hear about Coach Dye?" they asked.

"No, what about him?"

"He killed his wife Sunday morning?"

We knew a joke was coming on, but we played along.

"OK, *why* did Coach Dye kill his wife?"

"Because when he woke up and asked her what time it was, she said, 'Twenty to seven.'"

September 20

Good news and bad news today.

Good news first.

Beating Ole Miss so easily has moved us up from No. 12 to No. 6 in The Associated Press poll. Auburn, the team *Playboy* picked to win it all, fell to No. 11. But it's still early in the season yet, and a lot can happen between now and January 1.

Now for the bad news.

I stood on the sidelines again today and watched Joe Smith take my place at practice. As if that wasn't bad enough, I later read a story in the *Birmingham News* which quoted Coach Perkins as saying that I was "definitely out" of Saturday's game with Vandy. This is news to me. But since Stan Gay was also listed as being out of the lineup and Stan is practicing with bruised ribs, I can only assume that this is merely propaganda for Vandy scouts.

But that's only half the story.

I read further and discovered that Coach Perkins says he is considering moving Greg Richardson to split end (my position) because, and I quote, "Split end is easier to learn."

Easier to learn? Who does he think he's kidding? Maybe I'm just being paranoid again, but it seems to me that Coach Perkins is just looking for an excuse to get Greg into the game as a starter. I can't blame Coach Perkins for that. Greg is a good player and he *should* play, but not at the expense of experienced seniors with equal talent.

There appears to be a definite trend developing here. Coach Perkins has not only shown that he isn't afraid to play freshmen, but to prefer them. I didn't realize just how much until I saw today's *Tuscaloosa News*. For there, in living color, was a huge picture of all the freshmen who have already seen action in just two games. There were 11 of them—enough to make up their own football team. There was fullback Andrew Gilder, free safety Britton Cooper, linebacker Phillip Brown, flanker Mike Graham, nose guard Curt Jarvis, quarterback Mike Shula, linebacker Wayne Davis, linebacker Cornelius Bennett, place kicker Van Tiffin, halfback Kerry Goode, and of course, Richardson.

Next to the picture was a story quoting several of the freshmen. Most said they were surprised to be playing at all. Most would have been happy just to make the traveling squad. Instead, there seems to be a freshman in on every offensive and defensive play. Curt Jarvis played almost an entire half against Georgia Tech. Wayne Davis had nine tackles against Ole Miss and was named UPI lineman of the week. Cornelius Bennett has 16 individual tackles—tops on the team.

It's obvious that they are a good freshman class, probably the best since our class. They may even be better.

And we *are* winning. In the end, that's all that matters.

September 21

Hello again.

It took one heck of an acting job again, but I was able to

convince Coach Goostree to let me practice again today. My ankle has returned to its normal size and color, and that helped pursuade the Goose. Now, all I have to do is convince myself that my ankle doesn't hurt.

Since several people seem to have forgotten how tough Vanderbilt was last season, Coach Perkins took tonight's team meeting to remind them.

"This isn't the Vanderbilt team that Alabama used to beat 60-something to nothing," he said. "Don't you think for a second that they are. They are a good team now and they're getting better every year. That offense of theirs can score at any time. They come up with the big plays, the great plays because they believe that they can beat you.

"You've got to believe that you can come up with the great plays, too. You've got to picture them in your mind before you even go out there. Stop that drive! Cause that fumble! Do something great! Make it *mean* something to you."

I can't believe it—two whole paragraphs and not a single "standpoint" or "-wise."

And finally, a line from the most hated but best read sports columnist in the state—Paul Finebaum of the *Birmingham Post-Herald:* "Maybe now reality will come back to this campus. Maybe now Auburn fans will quit believing *Playboy* and go back to the *Farmers Almanac.*"

September 25
Bryant Hall
This is going to sound strange. We almost lost to Vanderbilt and I'm glad we did.

We haven't had what I call a real comeback since I've been here, and I was beginning to wonder if we could come back. We needed something to wake us up, to test our character and willingness to win. This game did all that and more. We went from trailing 17-0 in the first quarter to winning the game 44-24. People can talk about great comebacks in Alabama football history, about 1979 when Tennessee had Alabama down 17-0 but we came back to win 27-17. . .but as far as I'm concerned this comeback ranks with any of them.

Vandy came out with fire in their eyes, and before we could blink, they had a 17-point lead. We knew they were not afraid to pass on first down, but we never expected that they would go for the home run ball on the first play from scrimmage. But that's what they did. Vandy's Chuck Scott streaked down the left sideline and Kurt Page threw him a 59-yard pass for a touchdown. A lot of people are going to blame Rocky Colburn for letting Scott get by him, but it was something that couldn't be helped. We were in man-to-man coverage and Rocky had his man covered. Rocky lunged for Scott's legs, but he kicked his legs up and got loose for the score. The reason you have man-to man coverage in the first place is to put pressure on the quarterback and force him to throw a bad pass. But Page threw a perfect pass anyway, and any receiver will tell you that a perfect pass in man coverage is always to the receiver's advantage.

Anyway, we fumble on our first play, Vandy recovers and scores in five plays. Now, it's 14-0. We try again, but the drive dies. Malcolm Simmons punts and we back Vandy up their own 2-yard line. We figure we've got 'em where we want them, that we can get a fumble here and then score quickly. Instead, Carl Woods beats Freddie Robinson on a 47-yard pass. Now, Vandy's at mid-field and Freddie gets beat twice more. But then, our defensive line tightens and Freddie bats down a pass to stop the drive. Vandy settles for the wild possibility of making a 52-yard field goal attempt. Lo and behold, they do make it.

So now, it's 17-0 and there's just over three minutes left in the first quarter. I'm thinking that these new white helmets we're wearing are jinxed. We're getting desperate. I go out for a couple of long passes, but both times Walter Lewis has to rush his pass and overthrows me. The offensive linemen are getting ticked off at themselves because they can't keep Vandy off of Walter. I return to the huddle to hear Mike Adcock berating Hardy Walker. "Hardy, you better get your damn man this time!" Adcock screams. On the next play, Hardy takes his man out. Still, we aren't able to get anything going until just over 10 minutes into the second quarter. Malcolm Simmons' punt backs Vandy up to their own 6-yard line. This time, they *do* fumble and

Freddie Robinson recovers. After a big gainer by Ricky Moore and a couple of good runs by Linnie Patrick, Walter sneaks over for the score. Van Tiffin kicks the point after and we're down 17-7.

Patrick is still running wild on our next series and we're able to get down to Vandy's 16-yard line before we have to settle for Van's 33-yard field goal. It's good, and now the score is only 17-10. We're on a roll. Vandy nets minus 11 yards on its next possession, but we only have 24 seconds to score before the half ends. On the first play, I break across the middle, shake off a linebacker and catch a pass for 24 yards to bring us to Vandy's 11-yard line. On the very next play, Walter scrambles across for the score. Van kicks the point after and it's tied 17-17 as we head for the locker room, feeling lucky just to be alive.

Inside the locker room, Coach Henshaw is beside himself. He's clapping his hands and saying, "Great job, men! Great comeback!" That's when Coach Perkins burst through the doors screaming, "Don't you start telling them what a great job they've done, dammit! You better start telling them what the hell they're going to have to do to win this damn game! Coach Henshaw's eyes widen and he blushes as Coach Perkins turns his anger on us.

"I told you all damn week that Vanderbilt was a good team, but you didn't listen, did you?!! I told you and told you that they aren't just going to roll over just because you're Alabama! They are out there trying to win this damn game and they're kicking your butts! I told you they could, but you didn't believe me! Do you believe me now, dammit?! Do you believe me now?!!"

Just when we thought he was through, a manager approached him.

"Coach Perkins. . .?" the manager asked timidly.

Coach Perkins bristled. His face turned red and the tiny hairs on the nape of his neck stood at full attention.

"Get the hell away from me!" he roared, flailing his arms.

This set him off again and be began chewing us out all over again. It was the longest halftime I've ever been through. By the time the third quarter rolled around, I was ready to get out of there and get back on the field.

On the third play of the second half, Venson Elder intercepted Kurt Page's pass at the Vandy 30. Six plays later, we scored from the two. Van Tiffin kicked the extra point and we led

24-17. Vandy shanked a punt on its next possession, and when I caught a 13-yard pass on a post pattern, I could feel the momentum shifting our way. Leonard Coleman must have felt it too because he started hitting harder. Twice, he slugged me in the ribs while I was lying on the ground. I warned the referee, but he said he saw nothing. I repaid Coleman by cutting him down at the knees. But before I get off the ground, he kicks me in the head. This time the referee sees him.

Van Tiffin kicks a 28-yard field goal and we're on our way with a 27-17 lead. But Vandy puts together a long drive and scores to make it 27-24. I catch another 17-yard pass over the middle on our next possession, and Joe Carter scores on a six yard run. Tiffin kicks it to 34-24 and you can see it in the Vandy players' faces that they know they're licked. In the fourth quarter, Tiffin kicks another 39-yard field goal and we're up 37-24. And finally, Freddie Robinson intercepts another Page pass and Ricky Moore breaks loose on a 37-yard run for our last touchdown.

The locker room was a mad house after the game. We were giving high-five handshakes and patting ourselves on the back. We felt like we had really done something and we were pleased with ourselves. So was Coach Perkins.

"Great comeback, men," he said. "I had told you that Vanderbilt wasn't the team it used to be, and they almost beat you because you didn't believe me. But you came back and won a game that a lot of teams would've just tucked their heads between their legs and given up. You didn't. You made a lot of mistakes that we're going to have to work on next week, but I have to hand it to you—that was a great comeback."

I, for one, agree.

Get ready, Memphis State, you're next.

Homecoming week.

Usually I find homecoming week to be much ado about nothing. Even with all its parties and parades and hoopla, it's still the most overrated date on a college football schedule. Yet I find myself anxiously awaiting this weekend's game with Memphis State because I'll see my old friend, Greg Sanders from Murphy

High School in Mobile. Greg was the quarterback on my high school team. He made me look good by throwing plenty of passes my way, and I made him look good by catching them. It was a great arrangement.

But now, we're on opposite sides. Greg plays defensive back for Memphis State, and all indications are that I'll be going head to head with him Saturday. This is going to ruin our old arrangement. Greg may be a friend, but he's a competitor, too, and if he can beat me on a play, I'm sure he will give it all he's got. I just hope I can beat him.

September 27

I've said it before, but I'll say it again—I can't figure these coaches out. As I was walking out of the dressing room today, I saw Craig Turner looking at the depth chart and cussing to himself. Later, I saw why—Craig has been dropped to third team. He didn't play at all against Vandy and has carried the ball only eight times this whole season. At this point last season, he was "Touchdown" Turner and had scored five touchdowns. Looks like that fumble against Georgia Tech is not going to be forgotten soon.

Got a call from Greg Sanders tonight and we spent a half hour talking about old times. Naturally, we talked about the game, too. Greg admits that a 1-2 Memphis State team against a 3-0 Alabama team is probably a mismatch, but he would never admit that Memphis State would lose Saturday. Greg's too much of a competitor for that.

Instead, he talked about what Memphis State would try to do to win. He said that Coach Dockery had seen us play Vanderbilt and that he was impressed. He also said that Dockery felt like Freddie Robinson was a talented, but inconsistent, cornerback.

"Your backfield sounds like it's pretty young and inexperienced," Greg said. "Coach Dockery thinks we should take advantage of that inexperience and work Robinson quite a bit."

"But what did he say about me?" I asked.

"He said that you were a lot faster than most people think, that you had good hands, and that you could beat us deep if we don't watch out."

"Aw," I said. "He didn't say that."

"Yes, he did," Greg replied.

"I think you're just trying to set me up. You wouldn't do that to me, would you Greg?"

"You know me better than that. You just take it easy on us, OK?"

Sorry, pal, but we'll take you any way we can.

September 28

Coach Felker, who was put in charge of scouting Memphis State mainly because he coached there the last two years, gave us a warning while we were watching films today.

"I know these guys," he said, "and you'd better watch them. They're a dirty bunch. They'll start stuff with you. You gotta watch'em. You don't want to turn your back on them."

Jesse Bendross is pouting. He's been depressed ever since Saturday night when he didn't catch a single ball against Vanderbilt. He has caught only five passes for 95 yards this season, and it's bugging him. I know how he feels. This newfangled offense hasn't been that much different from the wishbone for us receivers. Through three games last year, I had caught five passes for 113 yards. This year I've caught seven for 124 yards, not much difference. Coach Felker keeps telling us to be patient, that the passes will come when the time is right. But we're all running thin on patience.

September 30

Paul Carruth tells me that his sister, Carla, has been elected homecoming queen for tomorrow's game. He's really proud of her.

When I was a freshman, I thought one of the grandest things about being a football player was the homecoming pep rally on Friday night. Just seeing the seniors standing up there on stage, being introduced to the audience, sent shivers down my spine. I couldn't wait to become a senior. Tonight, I got my chance to walk out on that stage. Know what I felt? Nothing.

I have my game face squarely in place now. I skipped all my Friday classes again, and now, I'm so wound up that I can't sleep. I just hope I don't oversleep like I did my sophomore year before we played Cincinnati. I was rooming with Darryl White then and we were both snoozing away when we heard this loud knocking on our door. I opened the door to find Butch Ellard, our assistant equipment manager, standing there with a look of horror on his face.

"You mean you guys aren't dressed yet?!" he exclaimed. "Man, don't you know the buses are about to leave for the stadium?!"

I flew off in a hundred different directions, pulling on my pants, putting on my shirt, looking around for my shoes. Within a matter of seconds, I was dressed and standing at the door, yelling for Darryl to hurry. He was still sitting on the edge of the bed fumbling with his socks.

"Don't worry about it, Joey," Darryl kept muttering. "Don't worry. We just gotta be cool about it. Gotta be cool."

When he finally got dressed, all three of us flew out the door like The Three Stooges. The buses were sitting there ready to roll with their engines at full idle. The first bus was the closest to us, and we made a bee line for it. But just as we started to get on, I caught a glimpse of Coach Bryant's houndstooth hat. We immediately reversed our direction and went straight to the third bus. If Coach Bryant saw us, he never said a word.

October 1

We probably short-circuited a half dozen of the old grads' pacemakers today, but we still won 44-13. This was a classic example of how *not* to play football. I'll spare you the gruesome details and just hit the high (and low) spots.

To start with, we fell behind 10-0 right off the bat. By halftime, we had cut it to 10-3 but it was still too close for Coach Perkins, who proceeded to give us another tongue-lashing in the locker room. He told us to "get off of our butts and get out there and win our second straight game in Bryant-Denny Stadium." So, we did. We scored 21 points in the third quarter (Memphis State got three) and 20 more in the fourth. The final three points came with just 31 seconds on a record 51-yard field goal by Van Tiffin.

The late field goal really took me by surprise, and I'm more than a little worried about what the fans might say about us going for three more points when we already had a 28-point lead. I don't know what Coach Perkins was thinking about when he called Van out to try the kick. When I saw Van walk onto the field, Kurt Schmissrauter nudged me and said, "What are we doing?!"

"I don't know," I said, "Maybe, Van's going to punt instead of Malcolm Simmons."

But then, Van kicked through the uprights, and we both rolled our eyes back. It was a terrible thing to do to any team, and we knew it. But we weren't about to say anything to Coach Perkins.

Along the way, I caught four passes for 50 yards and the tying touchdown to start the third quarter. And I gave Memphis State cornerback Donnie Elder such fits that he tried to pick a fight with me. I had just caught a pass and was walking back toward the huddle when Elder reached out and slapped me in the back of the head. The ref, of course, didn't see it but I spent the rest of the game doing everything I *legally* could to get back at him. So, Coach Felker was right—they *are* a dirty bunch. I wouldn't have had that problem with Greg, but they had moved him to the opposite side of the field, and I never met him once all day except to shake hands before the game started.

I was also humiliated by Coach Rader in front of 60,210 people and unjustifiably so. I ran a perfect route, but Walter was scrambling and he threw the ball late. So, when I ran to the sidelines, I got chewed out.

"What are you doing running a 13-yard route!" Coach Rader screamed. "That's supposed to be 16 yards! The quarterback hasn't got time to set up that quickly when you run a route like that.”

Again, I just stood there and took it, but I knew he was wrong.

Still, the fact remains that we are unbeaten after four games. And that’s a lot better than some people gave us credit for. Coach Perkins says that winning games like this will give him gray hair, but it’s even harder on us.

Paul Carruth watched the game from the stands and said that the fans spent the first half cussing us out and the second half pulling for us.

“I hate going to these games now,” Paul said. “You should’ve heard the way people are talking about the team. You guys are out there doing all you can to win, and they sit up there second-guessing and booing you. I tell you, Joey, I was ready to punch somebody out.”

I laughed and told him to take it easy.

“Yeah, you go ahead and laugh at me now,” Paul said, “But your time’s coming. Next year, *you’ll* have to sit up there and go through what I went through today.”

October 2

Game films today showed that the route Coach Rader had questioned I ran perfectly. It was 16 yards to the inch. Afterwards, Coach Rader apologized—in private.

Next up, Penn State.

Your’s truly has been named a game captain for this game, a game that will be nationally televised by CBS. How do I feel? Like I’m 10 feet tall.

With Penn State coming up, I find myself thinking more and more of Coach Bryant. During a water break last summer, Coach Bryant was walking up and down the sideline and cracking jokes. He didn’t realize that his fly was unzipped, and as he walked past us, everyone would snicker quietly. Finally Mark Jackson spoke up.

“Uh, Coach Bryant,” he said, “your fly is open.”

“Well, I’ll be danged,” Coach Bryant said, looking down and rezipping his pants. “I’m just glad I wasn’t somewhere that I had to wear a tuxedo.”

The worst trip in the world is the one to State College. The airport isn't big enough for our charter jet to land, so we had to fly into Lewiston and then take a two and one-half hour bus ride into State College. By the time we arrived at the hotel, our legs were in knots.

You can learn a lot about people on a two and one-half hour bus ride, though. For instance, there is a very definite seating order that seems to suit the players' individual personalities. The hell raisers, such as Linnie Patrick, Scott McRae, Jesse Bendross, Mark Jackson and David Valleto always head to the back of the bus where they can play cards, tell jokes and listen to music. I'm a middle-of-the-bus person myself. I like to sit quietly and either read my accounting book or just think about the game. Joe Dismuke, Gary Otten, Brent Sowell and Thornton Chandler are other middle-of-the-bus people. The front of the bus is occupied by the quiet, unassuming introverts such as Walter Lewis, Freddie Robinson and Van Tiffin. They never bother anybody.

I am reminded of the last time we came to Penn State. It was Coach Bryant's 314th career victory and tied him with Amos Alonzo Stagg as the winningest coach of all time. As memorable as that game was, however, what I remember most was the return flight. We were flying over this mountainous region in the middle of a thunderstorm. It was thundering and lightning was popping all around us. Occasionally, the plane would drop suddenly and everyone's face would turn white as a sheet. That was the only time I've ever really been scared in an airplane. Still, I had only one thought: "If we crash, Coach Bryant won't be able to break the record."

Had a heart-to-heart talk with Paul Fields tonight. And although he may not play another down for the University of Alabama, I'm convinced that he is the most courageous player I've ever known.

I was lying on my bed in the hotel room watching the television news when Paul returned from the quarterbacks' meeting.

"How'd it go tonight?" I asked him.

"It went okay," he said. "Looks like we'll be throwing a lot of passes tomorrow."

"Great!" I said. "It's about time."

Then I noticed that Paul wasn't smiling as usual. He looked bored, tired. He was wanting to play, too, but knew he probably wouldn't get the chance.

"Feeling left out, huh?" I asked him

"I sure am," he said, shaking his head. "But I'm getting used to it."

"How *do* you do it, Paul? How *can* you put up with being on the sidelines game after game?"

"It's not easy. You pray a lot. You work hard and hope somebody notices you. And if they don't, well, you just suck it up and try to help the team some other way."

"I can't worry about it," he went on. "If I worried about it, I'd probably go crazy. I think God is testing me right now. It's going to pay off some way down the road—it may be with my family, it might be with my job, it could be anything. I don't know what. But I'm going to learn something from this. I'm not going to let it bother me. I'm going to turn this around and learn something from it."

"Maybe," I said, "but I still don't see how you do it. I'd probably kill myself if I had to go through what you're going through. It really takes a special kind of person to handle that. I just wish I had in me whatever it is you have in you."

"Thanks, J.J. It's good to know somebody is behind me."

October 9
Tuscaloosa

As I've said before, one of the first rules you learn around this place is that you don't talk about game officials. It's probably a good rule and one that I try to live with. I don't even like to talk about officiating because no matter what you say, you always come off sounding like a sore loser.

First let me begin by saying that last Thursday Danny Holcombe, the perennial Jet and now assistant coach, told me that Coach Perkins was having a dispute over game officials with Penn State. Danny said that he heard that Donald Guman, the father of the Penn State running back who we stopped on the famous goal line stand in the Sugar Bowl, was going to be one of the game officials. Danny also said that Coach Perkins was trying to get Guman "scratched" from the game, but wasn't having much luck because the contract agreed that Penn State could select the game officials.

At the time, this little detail, although interesting, seemed unimportant and I brushed it aside. I figured that there was no way that one man could influence the outcome of a game played on national television. Boy, was I ever wrong.

Quite simply, we were robbed. The score was Penn State 34, Alabama 28. But that's not the whole story. The story is that we were tailing 34-7 going into the fourth quarter, but came back and had a chance to win the game in the final eight seconds. We were on Penn State's 4-yard line, fourth-and-goal, and trailing 34-28. All we needed was a touchdown and extra point to win.

Walter Lewis called for *Z fly 99,* a pass route with Jesse Bendross the intended receiver. The ball was snapped, Walter was blitzed and Jesse was covered. Walter scrambled free and saw Preston Gothard in the end zone directly behind me. The ball went over my head, and as I turned, I saw Preston clutching the ball with both hands in mid-air. When he fell into the end zone and I saw one ref signal a touchdown, I knew we had won the game. I ran to Preston and jumped up in his arms. I was waiting for the rest of the team to pile on. When they didn't, I knew something was wrong. I turned and saw Penn State players slapping one another on the back. Near the sidelines, I saw Mike Adcock standing in front of another referee, screaming at the top of his lungs with his fists balled up. I looked back at Preston and then we ran over to see what all the commotion was about.

The official had called the pass incomplete, saying that Preston had fallen out of the end zone.

"How can you say that?! How can you say that?!" Mike was bellowing as he bumped his chest against the referee. "How can you say that?! How can you say that?!"

Before I could decide whether to cry or to punch out the referee, Preston stuck the ball under his nose and was yelling, "See?! I got it! See?"

The next thing I knew, I was standing there along with Preston and Mike, shouting at the ref.

"That's it! That's it." I yelled. "Take the damn game away

from us. Go ahead, just *give* it to 'em!"

Ordinarily, any other referee would have thrown all three of us out of the game. But this guy didn't lift an eyebrow. He had blown the call and he knew it. He just stood there looking guilty.

As we were dressing after the game, Wayne Atcheson, our sports information director, walked up and whispered something in Coach Perkins' ear. As he listened, Coach Perkins' face grew redder and redder until, finally, he flung a paper cup down beside me and started yelling "Is that right?! Damn, that makes me mad! I want that checked out! I want to know if he's the one who made that call in the end zone. And I want to know if he's Mike Guman's father! I want to know that for sure!"

It wasn't Guman's father who made the call, though. It was some guy named O'Rourke, Jack O'Rourke. But it really doesn't matter who made the call—it was still a bad one. Unfortunately, our game films didn't have the proper angle to prove him wrong All I know is that I saw the play, and it was a bad call. I'll believe that until the day I die.

Considering the circumstances, Coach Perkins was remarkably calm today. The worst thing he did was revoke David Valletto's season tickets for the rest of the year. He said it was because of David's repeated curfew violations, but I wonder if it's not because David got burned on an 80-yard touchdown pass against Penn State.

"We've got to put this game behind us," Coach Perkins said. "We've got Tennessee next. Penn State's history now. Forget it."

That will be easier said than done.

October 12

Did I mention that it would be hard to forget the loss to Penn State? It's not just hard—it's impossible. Here it is four days later and people are still asking me about it. The newspapers are still filled with stories about the controversy over the pass play.

Doesn't anybody realize that Tennessee, our next opponent, is 3-2 and has the best overall defense in the whole Southeastern Conference?

Hello? Is anybody out there listening?

David Valletto's mistake against Penn State has cost him more than just game tickets—it's cost him his starting job. Today,

David joined the ever growing cast of past superstars on the third team roster. He has been replaced by Britton Cooper, a freshman. Craig Turner is still living in exile on the third team, while Andrew Gilder, another freshman, takes over his old job. Joe Carter isn't there yet, but might as well be for all the attention they're giving him. Joe has been relegated to special team duty while Kerry Goode, still another freshman, will start at halfback against Tennessee.

I remember when experience counted for something.

One picture is worth a thousand words. And so, when Coach Donahue switched on the projector tonight and we saw a high school team playing on the screen, we immediately started laughing.

"Ha, ha, ha," we said. "I think you've got the wrong film in there, Coach."

"Oh, doggone it," Coach Donahue said. "But let's watch it anyway."

The projector whirred on as we watched these two high school games battle it out on the silver screen.

"Notice anything special about that defensive team?" Coach Perkins asked.

There was something in his voice that let us know that there was supposed to be something different, but we couldn't figure it out. We looked a little closer.

Finally, Mike Adcock saw what Coach Perkins was talking about.

"Yeah!" said Mike. "It's the nose guard!"

"Well," said Coach Perkins, "what about him?"

"He's got only one leg!"

"That's right," said Coach Perkins, "Look at him go!"

So we sat there and watched this one-legged nose guard play his heart out on every play and try to make tackles that most people would've given up on. Nothing else had to be said. Coach Perkins had made his point.

October 15

"There are three ways to lose a game." Coach Perkins said today. "One is to sit on your butt and not do a damn thing.

Another is to beat yourself with silly mistakes, fumbles and penalties. And still another is to get into a scoring contest with somebody and the other team is the last one to get the ball. That last way is how you lost today."

Actually, I wasn't sure how we lost. All I know is that I caught five passes for 91 yards and a touchdown, we were leading 24-17 at the half, and we ended up losing 41-34. In between, I saw our defense give up two 80-yard touchdown passes (that makes three 80-yarders in two games) and I saw Johnnie Jones run 66 yards virtually untouched with three minutes left to play to score the winning touchdown.

So now, we're 4-2 overall and it's very unlikely that we can win a national championship this year. Unlikely, but not impossible.

Randy Edwards is taking it really hard. After we got back to the dorm, Randy roamed around the hallways apologizing to every offensive player he could find.

"Man, I'm sorry," he said. "It's our fault. The defense lost this one. If you guys can score 34 points, there's no reason we should lose. It's our fault. We just haven't played together long enough. We let you down."

Without realizing it, Randy had pinpointed our entire problem in one short sentence—"we just haven't played together long enough." At least, that's what I think our problem is. Randy and Stan Gay were the only returning starters on the field at one point today, while six were freshmen. Six! It's hard to tell your defense how important it is to stop Tennessee when they were playing for Podunk High School just a year ago.

I thought I was the only one who felt this way. And to tell you the truth, I felt guilty for even thinking it. But as it turns out, I'm not alone. A lot of the seniors are getting teed off about so many freshmen getting playing time while experienced players ride the bench. Losing this game just sort of brings it to a head.

Tonight, behind the safety of closed doors, we aired our gripes. The conversation went something like this:

Paul Carruth: "I really felt for you guys today. You played a great game on offense, but the defense just couldn't hold 'em back. There just weren't any experienced people out there . . .all those freshmen."

Paul Fields: "I can't understand why Coach Perkins is doing

this. We've got all these experienced people and he keeps putting freshmen in."

Me: "How many freshmen did play today anyway?"

Kurt Schmissrauter: "I don't know how many there were, but they kept running them in and out all day long. Randy said he looked up in the huddle once and there were six freshmen in there with him. He said he didn't even know three of them."

Me: "We definitely need more experience in there. Heck, Kurt you should be playing more than you are."

Kurt Schmissrauter: "I can't do anything about that. But I'll tell you one thing, if I hadn't made the traveling squad to this game, I would've quit. I've been talking to my Dad about it, but he says to go ahead and sweat it out. He says, "There's nothing you can do about it, so just go ahead and have fun. You can't go through your last year pissed off at everybody.' Well, I'm just tired of worrying myself about it. Screw it—let's go get a keg."

October 16

I was expecting Coach Perkins to jump all over the defense at today's meeting. Instead, he crawled all over the offense.

"It's not all the defense's fault we lost," he said. "You guys could have helped, too. Don't you think you could have scored at least one more touchdown?"

I don't think he was serious, though. Because after the offense finished meeting, the defense stayed. And they were still there when I returned from a fishing trip late this afternoon.

What we need is a vacation. Lucky for us, we have an open date before we play Mississippi State.

October 25

Hello again.

A few days' rest helped soothe the sting of two straight losses, but it hasn't changed Coach Perkins' thinking very much. He's still convinced that freshmen are the key to winning, and he's tabbed five—Britton Cooper, Ricky Thomas, Wayne Davis, Curt Jarvis and Cornelius Bennett—to start Saturday against Mississippi State. And that's just the defense!

David Valletto looked at the depth chart again today and said, "Well, maybe I'll get to play in the spring game next year."

And during a break in practice today, Mike Adcock and I looked to the far end of the practice field where we saw Craig Turner simply going through the motions of practice. Third team has killed his spirit.

"He's too good to be down there," Mike said.

"Yeah, I know."

October 28

Kurt Schmissrauter and I walked down to the mail box in Bryant Hall today, and Kurt began sorting through the mail, looking for any letters he might have received. The only mail he could find was addressed to me.

"Joey Jones, Joey Jones, Joey Jones," he said as he thumbed through a stack of mail. "Joey Jones. . .heck, there's no sense in me looking—they're all for you!"

I attribute this sudden increase in fan mail to the fact that I will turn 21 tomorrow. I don't know how fans find out when my birthday is, but they do. I've received cards from Montana and Ohio, Texas and Arkansas. . .places I've never even heard of. Some fans such as Wanda Wade of Headland and Mandy Davidson of Talladega write every week. Both sent cards today.

Thanks, kids, keep those cards and letters coming.

My Mom, aunt and uncle and some friends from Mobile stopped by my hotel room tonight and I celebrated my 21st birthday for the 21st time this week. Walter Lewis stopped by for a piece of birthday cake at which time Mom saw fit to remind Walter, "You better be good to my little boy tomorrow, Walter. . . . .be sure you throw him plenty of passes."

Walter smiled and said, "Yes, ma'am."

October 29

Now *that's* what I call a birthday party!

I caught seven passes for 94 yards, the defense forced

Mississippi State into settling for four field goals and only one touchdown, and we won 35-18. One of my catches came on a double slant when Walter Lewis was blitzed and the pass sailed directly between Greg Richardson and myself. Either of us could have caught it, but I claimed seniors' privilege and stole it right out from under Greg's nose.

"Man, I'm sure glad you caught that ball," Greg said later.

"Well, Greg," I said, "I'm a little older than you."

To top it all off, the crowd sang "Happy Birthday" to me.

Nothing is going to spoil this day. . .

October 30

A little food for thought at the breakfast table. . .

My friend Willie Goyne, who had come up from Mobile for the game and spent the night in Tuscaloosa, called this morning to invite me and Britton Cooper, the freshman safety from Mobile, to join him and another friend, Jimmy Mills, for breakfast. As much as I like Britton, I resented him, in a sense, for tagging along because I had always considered Willie and Jimmy to be *my* friends and I didn't want to share them with a freshman.

But then, we got to talking about the game and how the freshmen have made such an impact on our season. And I began to see Britton in a different light.

"Britton, did you ever expect to play this much in your freshman year?" Jimmy asked.

"No sir," said Britton. "When I first got here, I would've been happy just to dress out. Now, they're depending on me to start. Nobody's more surprised than I am."

That's when it hit me. 'Dern,' I thought, 'That's exactly how I felt when I was a freshman!'

You can't blame a guy for wanting to play.

November 2

There is only one place on earth that is noisier than LSU's Tiger Stadium on a Saturday afternoon in November—and that's Thomas Field on a Wednesday afternoon before the LSU game. Coach Perkins, borrowing one of Coach Bryant's old tricks, thought it would be a good idea if we prepared ourselves for the crowd noise in Tiger Stadium. So, he pulled the old sound system out of moth balls today and we practiced with the sound of recorded crowed noise echoing all across campus.

This is the first time we have used the old sound system since our season opener at Baton Rouge in 1981. The fans began arriving early for that game and the stadium was half filled by the time we took our usual pre-game walk around the field. As we walked along in our street clothes, inspecting the field for rocks and drainage holes, the fans began booing us. Some threw paper cups; others threw empty whiskey bottles. The longer we walked, the rowdier the fans became. Suddenly, the noise died down and the throwing stopped. I turned to see why, and there, walking 30 yards behind me, was Coach Bryant blowing kisses to the crowd and smiling all the way.

Willard Scissum, the offensive tackle from Huntsville, hasn't played since he hurt his foot in the Penn State game. So when I saw him standing in the hallway outside Paul Fields' room today, I asked him about it.

"When are you going to stop faking that injury and get back out there and help us?" I asked jokingly.

"Injury? What injury?" Willard said. "I'm not hurt. My foot is fine . . . has been for over a week. They just won't let me play."

Leave it up to me to put somebody else's foot in my mouth. . .

November 5

Victory is never so sweet as when it is soaked with revenge. We got our revenge on LSU today. And while we may not have physically pounded them as they did us last year, they will be awfully sore tomorrow morning. The score was 32-26 and the only drawback was that we once again gave up an 80-yard touchdown pass on LSU's first play. *Why do we keep doing this?*

As for myself, well, I caught only one pass for six yards. But it was a difficult catch on the end line and I still managed to keep my foot in bounds for a touchdown. I can't wait to see the television replay.

As much as I enjoyed winning again, I also enjoyed seeing

Bruce Davis, my former roomie from Bryant Hall. Bruce is now enrolled as a student at LSU, but he was still wearing crimson and white. He said he sat in the LSU student section pulling for us all the way and the students poured drinks all over him.

"But," he said, "it was worth it."

Once a Tider, always a Tider.

November 6

Coach Mike DuBose was always a Tider, too.

Coach DuBose, who coaches defensive ends, was a defensive end here in the early 1970's but spent last season at Southern Mississippi under Coach Jim Carmody. Apparently, Coach DuBose isn't too proud of that.

We were sitting in the projection room today, waiting for the scouting report on Southern Miss when Coach DuBose stormed into the room looking as if he was ready to kill someone.

"I was on the opposite side of the field last year when Southern Miss beat you guys in Tuscaloosa," he said gruffly. "And after that game, they printed up these. . .these. . .bumper stickers."

He paused, reached into his notebook and pulled out a bumper sticker which read, *'We Retired The Bear, 38-29.'* As he held the sticker up for us to see, Coach DuBose's face reddened and he gritted his teeth.

"After Coach Bryant died," he said, "I went to the funeral. But when I came back from the funeral, I stopped by to see Coach Carmody. And there, still stuck on Coach Carmody's desk, was one of these. . .these stickers.

"The man didn't have the *decency* to take that sticker off his desk. . .If that doesn't piss you off, nothing will! I don't know about you, but that makes me *damn* mad, that the man didn't have the *decency* to take this kind of *trash* off his desk!"

Coach DuBose stood there quivering with anger for a second, then threw the sticker back into his notebook.

"Now," he said, "let's talk about what we're gonna do to beat these guys. . ."

November 9

Was Southern Miss really responsible for Coach Bryant's retirement? Or are we to blame?

I've often wondered.

At any rate, Coach Perkins says that the loss to Southern Miss definitely had an unnerving effect on Coach Bryant.

"I was sitting with Coach Bryant in his office two days after the Southern Miss game last year," Coach Perkins said. "He didn't seem like the same man. He was a tired, battered man. He was beaten. It hurt me to see him like that. . .the loss had taken everything out of him."

Bowl rumors are beginning to fly. Everybody's guessing where we will be going. Some say the Liberty Bowl again, others say the Fiesta Bowl. And still others are talking about the Aloha Bowl, the Sun Bowl, and the Hall of Fame. But at this stage only one thing is for certain—we've got to win Saturday.

November 12

We retired Southern Miss today.

They returned the opening kickoff 96 yards to our 4-yard line where they began hurling insults at our defensive line. The most polite thing they said was, "We're gonna kill you!" Instead, Southern Miss folded like a tent. After four straight plays, all they had to show for that long kickoff return was Jon Hand's foot prints across their chests. We took over and marched 95 yards for a touchdown.

We won 28-16, but it wasn't a rout. They did a good job of shutting down our passing game and for the first time, I didn't catch a pass. Even Jesse Bendross was shut out after catching four passes in the first half.

But. . .we won. . .we're 7-2. . .and the bowl scouts were watching. What more can you ask for?

November 13

We could ask for Christmas in Hawaii. In fact, we did.

The December 26 Aloha Bowl was one of our choices when

the seniors met today to vote on which bowl game we would attend. Only it wasn't much of a vote.

"Since we're not playing for a national championship," Mike McQueen, our spokesman, said, "we'd like to go to the Aloha Bowl. A lot of us have never been to Hawaii and may never get that chance again."

"No," Coach Perkins said, "you don't want to go there. I've talked to one of the Washington coaches and he said the trip wasn't what you would expect. Washington went there last year and he said it wasn't much of a trip.

"If it *was* a great trip, I'd say, 'Heck, yeah! Let's go!' But since it doesn't seem like that good a trip, I can't see us spending that much money on it."

"The best option," he went on, "we have is the Sun Bowl. Everybody I've talked to has really been high on that bowl. The people there treat you right and there's a good chance that we can play SMU. If it is SMU, then that will give us a chance to play a team ranked in the top 10 and we can see if we have enough in us to beat a team of their stature.

"If that's what you want to do, I'll call 'em up and let 'em know your decision."

We considered the options. . .Sun Bowl, huh? El Paso, Texas. . . against SMU. . .on Christmas Eve. . .home for Christmas.

Home for Christmas.

"Call 'em," we said. "We'll take the Sun Bowl."

"All right," said Coach Perkins. "Sun Bowl it is."

November 15

One of my favorite pastimes is checking the sports pages for the weekly Southeastern Conference statistics just to see how well (or how poorly) I'm doing in relation to my peers.

Today's *Tuscaloosa News* shows that I have caught 29 passes for 430 yards and four touchdowns, an average of 14.8 yards per catch. Considering I only caught 25 passes all of last year, this isn't all that bad. But since the SEC ranks receivers on the average number of catches per game, I only rank sixth in the conference with an average of 3.2 catches per game.

The really lucky ones are the receivers for teams that pass a lot. For example, Vandy's Keith Edwards has caught 90 passes for 837 yards, an average of 9.3 yards per catch and 9.0 catches per game. Vandy's Chuck Scott is next with 66 catches for 924 yards and an average of 14.0 yards per catch and 6.6 catches per game.

Those are the kind of numbers a receiver dreams about. But if I had to wear a Vandy uniform to do it, I'd say "Thanks, but no thanks."

Thanks to television, our game with Boston College is still 10 days away. And although Coach Perkins has given us the last two days off, it can get pretty boring around Bryant Hall.

One of the ways we fight this boredom is by holding late-night knee football games in the hallway outside our dorm rooms. Knee football is one the greatest games ever invented. It's a lot of fun and it's really quite simple. All you need is a pair of rolled-up socks (preferably clean) to serve as your football, adhesive tape on the carpet to serve as yard markers, and plenty of imagination. It also helps to have two strong knees since all running, blocking and tackling must be done while on your knees.

Tonight, Mike Adcock and I were playing Doug Vickers and Mike White for the mythical World Knee Football Championship when the game was suddenly called on account of noise. I was just getting ready to make a towering dive over my lineman for a touchdown when Coach Rutledge appeared at the top of the stairs wearing nothing but his pants. We had obviously aroused him from his sleep.

"What's going on up here?!" Coach Rutledge said. "My goodness. . .don't you realize it's almost one o'clock in the morning?

"Let's hold it down some, please! You are making so much racket that I can't sleep for hearing your knees banging on the ceiling! Just quieten it down some—please!"

November 17

It's amazing how winning can influence a team's morale. Now that we've won two straight and have a good chance of finishing the year with a 10-2 record, the team now feels more relaxed than it has at any time since the season began.

Even "The Great Freshman Controversy" (known only to us seniors) has fizzled out. The starting lineup is still basically the same, but it's been more than two weeks since I've heard any disparaging remarks about a freshman. Resentment has turned to acceptance; acceptance to admiration.

It's like Paul Trodd, our senior placekicker from England, said after watching freshman placekicker Van Tiffin kick his 37th PAT of the season against Southern Miss: "I guess this skinny leg just 'ain't got enough to beat 'im out."

November 18

Nasty rumor going around that Coach Rutledge has been hanging around one of our local nightspots, trying to find out who's naughty or nice and then reporting what he sees to Coach Perkins. I don't know whether this is true, but I do know that Kerry Goode declined an invitation to go drinking with some of the older guys tonight.

"Uh uh! No way!" Kerry said. "I ain't going to that place no more! Coach Perkins told me to stay away from there and that's what I'm gonna do!"

November 20

Today, one day after bowl invitations were officially made official, Hardy Walker picked up a newspaper and said, "Hey, Joey! Didn't you say a Washington coach told Coach Perkins that the Aloha Bowl was a bad trip?"

"Yeah," I replied, "That's what Coach Perkins said. Why?"

"Oh, no reason. . .it just says here that Washington has accepted an invitation to play Penn State in the Aloha Bowl."

Aaaarrrgh!

Go ahead, ask. Everybody else has. Ask me why we decided to go to the Sun Bowl rather than the Fiesta. OK, I'll tell you. In the first place, the Fiesta Bowl thought it would be too risky to invite us because we might lose to Boston College and Auburn. In the second place, who cares what the Fiesta Bowl thinks? The Fiesta is considered a major bowl only because it is played January 2. The Sun Bowl is considered a minor bowl because it is played on December 24. But which is more important—when and where you play or *who* you play? I should think the latter.

When we get to the Sun Bowl, we'll be facing an SMU team that is now 9-and-1 and ranked sixth in the nation. We are 7-and-2 and ranked 13th.

So what does the Fiesta Bowl have? I'll tell you. The Fiesta has 8-and-3 Ohio State (ranked 14th) against 8-2-and-1 Pittsburgh (ranked 16th).

Now which is the *minor* bowl?

November 23

As I was standing on the practice field shivering in the cold today, I thought to myself, 'Just once. . .just once I'd like to see Alabama tell CBS television where to put their cameras.' But I know it won't happen. TV has all colleges over a barrel. Anything they want, they get. CBS wanted us to change the Boston College game from October 22 to this Friday, so we did. And now, we're out there freezing our buns off and thinking about how cold it will be in Foxboro, Mass., on Thanksgiving Day and the day after.

"It won't be *that* cold," Coach Perkins said. "When I was with the Giants and we played the Patriots there in November, it was 65 or 70 degrees.'

November 26

Sixty-five to seventy degrees, huh?

Would you believe 44 degrees, 20-mph winds, and rain, sleet and snow all at the same time? You better believe it because that's all we got in Sullivan Stadium yesterday. You may have seen the game on TV. Then again, you may not have—there was a power failure that permanently put the scoreboard out of commission and caused CBS to temporarily lose its picture. Worst of all, we lost the game. Boston College beat us 20-13 after we had carried a 13-6 lead into the fourth quarter.

I have never been so miserable. I spent most of the afternoon doing nothing but blocking. As it turned out, that was just as well. My hands were so numb I couldn't have caught anything anyway. My head wasn't in the game either. Near the end of the first half, we drove to the Boston 1-yard line and I came out of the game because we were going to the two tight end alignment. I ran immediately to the heaters on the sidelines to warm my hands. The next thing I knew Walter Lewis had fumbled the snap, the ball was back on the 8-yard line, and everyone was yelling, "Jones?! Where's Jones?! Jones get out there!" Two plays later, we had to settle for field goal attempt and I returned to the sidelines where Coach Perkins chewed me up one side and down the other.

"Always!" he shouted. "Always have your mind on the game!"

I wanted to say, "But, Coach, I've never done that before!" But I didn't think that was the appropriate time so I just let it pass.

As cold as it was outside, Coach Perkins kept things pretty hot in the locker room after the game. We were sitting there with our heads hanging between our knees, feeling sorry for ourselves. On the other side of the wall, you could hear Boston College players yelling and singing.

"Don't you hang your heads!" Coach Perkins bellowed. "Pull your heads up from there and listen to that! You hear that?" They deserve that! That's the taste of victory!"

The taste of defeat is coming back home and hearing your fans say that you have grown accustomed to losing. Nonsense. Just because we don't return home with tears in our eyes and a crutch under both arms doesn't mean that we're not hurting. We are.

So, pardon me if I don't shed a tear for Boston College. We have Auburn coming up in a few days, and there's no time for crying.

November 28

A slip of the lip can sink a ship, and a bad word spoken can get your ribs broken.

One thing you never want to do during such a crucial period as Auburn week is to incite the opponent—especially if they are a five and half point favorite. One wayward word can turn a close football game into a rout.

So what did we find in yesterday's *Birmingham News* but a story by Don Kausler with headlines that scream, "Tide tired of hearing about Auburn?" Actually, we *are* tired of hearing about them, but we'd rather they not know that until Saturday.

Sometimes, though, you get so caught up in the rivalry that you forget what you're saying and to whom you are talking.

For example, here are some of the zingers we provided Kausler:

From Jesse Bendross: "We've been hearing a lot about Auburn. I'm tired of hearing about them, to be honest. I think they've had a couple of lucky breaks. I felt Georgia had them whipped all over the field, and Florida, too."

From Mike Rodriquez: "I don't like Auburn. We want to beat them bad. Too bad to imagine. . ."

Naturally, this sparked another lecture from Coach Perkins on press relations.

"We need to watch what we're saying this week," he said. "Don't go shooting your mouth off to the press. Let's show some class!"

Coach Perkins didn't call any names, but Jesse had gotten the message.

"Damn!" Jesse said. "I ain't talking to any more reporters. If I haven't got anything good to say, I just won't say anything at all."

Actually, practice went surprisingly well. It was a hard practice and all indications are that it's about to get even harder this week. Coach Perkins made that clear after we finished up.

"Tell your wives, tell your girlfriends, tell the reporters—tell 'em all that you don't have any time for them this week," he said. "Because this week you belong to me!"

Although Auburn is 9-1 and has clinched a spot in the Sugar Bowl against Michigan, it should be pointed out that they are still not the Southeastern Conference champions. They are now 5-0 in SEC play, while we are 4-1. And if (or should I say, *when*) we beat them, they will have to share the SEC title with both Georgia and us. Share and share alike, I always say.

It should also be pointed out that Jesse's untimely remarks are only a result of his enthusiasm. In fact, he is so hyped up about this game that he reported to practice today with his head shaved.

November 29

A poster-sized sympathy card in the mail from Auburn today. It was addressed to the entire Alabama football team. Its message was simple: "We're Gonna Kick Your Ass!" Below that were the supposed signatures of Auburn football players. Nobody believes this card is for real. It's probably one of our own alumni playing mind games with us.

November 30

So here it is, four days before the big game and I can't think of anything to talk about. Last year, I talked too much and Auburn beat us. I talked too much after they beat us, too. I sounded like a sore loser. I *was* a sore loser. Auburn does that to me.

I guess that's why I found myself getting mad tonight when the coaches showed us an Auburn recruiting film. They called it "Eye of the Tiger" and it was filled with highlights from last year's game. By the time the film ended, I had almost bitten my tongue in two.

Coach Perkins says that if that film made us angry, it should have. He says that all the great state universities traditionally have the best football teams. And he believes it should stay that way.

Just when I was beginning to think that nobody would want a 5-foot-9 wide receiver, I received word today that I have been selected to play in the East-West All-Star Game in January. Friends in Mobile have already told me that I would be chosen for the Senior Bowl game, but I thought that was just because they wanted a hometown boy there as a gate attraction. But the East-West Game? Maybe, I'm not so bad after all. . .

December 1

Confidence is at a peak right now. Practice has gone beautifully this week, and I'm beginning to see that fire in Randy Edwards' eyes again. It's that same fire I saw in him last year as the Auburn game approached.

Coach Perkins has much the same look in his eyes. When someone mentions Auburn, he looks as if he just bit into a lemon.

"I hate to think I hate anybody," Coach Perkins was quoted as saying in today's *Tuscaloosa News*. "I don't particularly like Auburn. I can't lie. I think the feeling is mutual."

With that in mind, I'm going to indulge myself and tell just one Auburn joke this year. Here it is:

Man walks into store and tells the clerk, "I want an orange and blue wardrobe. I want a blue hat with an orange head band. I want a blue suit with orange buttons. I want an orange vest with blue buttons. I want a blue shirt with orange stripes. I want an orange tie with blue polka dots. I want blue shoes with orange laces and I want orange socks with blue stripes. Spare no expense."

"My, my," said the storekeeper, "you must be an Auburn fan."

"Yes," the man said proudly. "How did you guess?"

"Easy," said the storekeeper. "This is a *hardware* store!"

December 2
Birmingham

One of the student assistants in the Sports Information Department made a trip to Auburn earlier this week and purchased a whole bag full of Auburn paraphenalia—shirts, T-shirts, bumper stickers. He figures that if we wear these things, it will somehow psyche us up more for the game.

He wanted to give me a T-shirt that read, "Auburn Tigers" across the chest. I declined his offer. I've got my pride.

December 19
Tuscaloosa

The Auburn game? I thought you would never ask.
They won.

We lost.
Next question, please.

December 23
El Paso, Texas

I've never been much of a Marty Robbins fan, but I do love it here in the old border town of El Paso. You have the mountains on one side and the lights of Juarez, Mexico, glittering across the bridge on the other. You can see for miles, and it gives you a wonderful sense of freedom.

Some Southern Methodist players made a big deal out of having to come here. One defensive back, Fred Nichols, was quoted as saying, "El Paso, pitiful town." But I think their disgust was not so much with the town as it was with the major bowls who passed them by despite their 10-1 record and No. 6 ranking. Heaven knows, they seem to be enjoying it here now.

In fact, SMU has probably seen more of El Paso than we have. We have had a 1:30 curfew here every night and even that will be cut back to midnight tonight. SMU, on the other hand, hasn't had a curfew all week. Their only requirement is that they show up in time for practice sober. And from what I have heard, some have had trouble just doing that.

We are having fun, though. We've visited a few clubs, went shopping in Juarez, and toured a local boot factory. Still, our top priority is to win this game. For the seniors, myself included, this will be it—our last chance to show the fans that we can win and beat a nationally-ranked team. Anything else is secondary.

Nothing draws a team together as does the last game of the season. You get all choked up over little things like a handshake or a pat on the back. You get sentimental. You reminisce. And you talk about the future. Most of all, you feel time slipping away from you. . .and you know that the next time you take off that crimson jersey, it will be the last. It's a scary thought and it makes me more than a little sad.

December 24

Dear Santa,

Thanks for the Christmas gift. We beat SMU and beat 'em

good—28-7—and it was never in doubt. We led all the way. I caught only two passes for 36 yards, but one of those was for 19 yards and our final touchdown of the season. That was a nice sendoff. I tried to fight back the tears as the fans counted down the final 10 seconds of the game, but couldn't. The tears came anyway.

Afterwards, in the locker room, Coach Perkins walked around to every player and shook their hands. When he reached me, he shook my hand firmly and looked me straight in the eye.

"I've enjoyed having you, Joey," he said. "We're going to miss you."

"Thanks, Coach," I said. "I just wish we could have won the national title for you. I appreciate everything you've done. You did a good job in a very difficult situation. Good luck to you. I wish you the best."

I meant it, too.

Epilogue

New Year's Day, 1984

It is said that New Year's Day is for ringing out the old and ringing in the new. That is exactly what the Alabama Crimson Tide did during the fall and winter of 1983 when we were caught in the change from Coach Paul "Bear" Bryant to Coach Ray Perkins.

For me, the transition was a difficult one. For others, maybe it was not as difficult.

There were a number of reasons why I refused to accept Coach Perkins as my new leader. All of them seem quite foolish now. Several of us (maybe even most of us?) didn't like the way he talked. We didn't like the way he dressed. We didn't even like the way he combed his hair. Most of all, we didn't like *that* look—the icy stare that made you feel three inches tall. Behind his back, we called him "Businessman." To his face, he was always "Sir."

Slowly, we began to accept the inevitable. He was our coach, we his players. He would be here long after we were gone. Once we realized that he was for us, not against us, things went smoother. We adjusted to his habits and he adjusted to ours.

As the season progressed and we saw freshmen taking over roles traditionally held by upper classmen, we became resentful toward him. We felt that older players should be seeing more action by right of seniority. We blamed freshman immaturity for our losses and mistakes. But now, I see the immaturity was our own. Coach Perkins was only trying to build for the future. Just as Coach Bryant used to say, he was just "trying to win the game."

The biggest knock against Coach Perkins is that he is not Coach Bryant. He never will be. Nor will anyone else match the accomplishments of Coach Bryant. As soon as everyone realizes this and accepts it, the better off Alabama football will be.

I don't know what lies ahead for Alabama football. I can't predict the future. But I do know that Ray Perkins is a good coach and a good man. With him, Alabama football is in good hands.

EDITOR'S NOTES

Joey Jones completed his final season at the University of Alabama with 33 pass receptions for 504 yards and six touchdowns. On January 7, playing in the East-West Shriners Game against such greats as Nebraska's Turner Gill and Irving Fryar, Jones scored on a 45-yard touchdown pass and a 7-yard run to lead the East to a 27-19 victory. For his efforts, Jones was voted the game's Most Valuable Player. The following week Jones was back in his hometown of Mobile, catching four passes for 83 yards to help the South take a 21-20 victory over the North in the Senior Bowl.

On January 20, 1984, Joey Jones signed a three-year contract with the Birmingham Stallions of the United States Football League. In his first season as a pro, he caught 28 passes for 610 yards and 6 touchdowns as the Stallions posted a 15-5 record, won the Southern Division title and reached the USFL's Eastern Conference playoffs. In 1985, Jones and the Stallions were at it again. This time, Jones reeled in 52 passes for 897 yards and 8 touchdowns as the Stallions rolled to a 14-5 record before losing to defending champion Baltimore in the USFL semifinals.